CALLED & ACCOUNTABLE

CALLED & ACCOUNTABLE

GOD'S PURPOSE FOR EVERY BELIEVER

BY HENRY T. BLACKABY

AND KERRY L. SKINNER

New Hope Publishers

Birmingham, Alabama

New Hope Publishers
P. O. Box 12065
Birmingham, AL 35202-2065
www.newhopepubl.com

Library of Congress Cataloging-in-Publication Data
Blackaby, Henry T., 1935-
Called and accountable : God's purpose for every believer / by Henry T. Blackaby and Kerry L. Skinner.
p. cm.
ISBN 1-56309-723-0
1. Vocation—Christianity. I. Skinner, Kerry L., 1955- II. Title.
BV4740 .B57 2002
248.4—dc21

2002003748

Unless otherwise noted, Old Testament Scripture quotations are taken from the New King James Version (NKJV). Copyright© 1979, 1980, 1982 by Thomas Nelson, Inc. Used by permission. All rights reserved.

Unless otherwise noted, New Testament Scripture quotations are taken from the Holman Christian Standard Bible (HCSB). Copyright© 2000 by Holman Bible Publishers. Used by permission.

Scripture quotations marked (Amplified) are taken from the Amplified Bible, Old Testament, copyright© 1965, 1987 by the Zondervan Corporation. The Amplified Bible, New Testament, copyright© 1954, 1958, 1987 by the Lockman Foundation. Used by permission.

Scripture quotations marked (NIV) are taken from the HOLY BIBLE NEW INTERNATIONAL VERSION®. NIV®. Copyright© 1973, 1978, 1984 by International Bible Society. Used by permission of Zondervan. All rights reserved.

Cover design by Righteous Planet
ISBN: 1-56309-723-0
N024120 • 802 • 50M2

DEDICATION

To my uncle and his wife, Lorimer and Olive Baker,

who faithfully served as missionaries in Manchuria, China,

working with Jonathan Goforth during the great Shantung Revival,

and who baptized me as a nine-year-old boy and later became

my pastor when God called me into the ministry.

HENRY T. BLACKABY

TABLE OF CONTENTS

ABOUT THE AUTHORS

HENRY T. BLACKABY

Henry T. Blackaby has spent his life in ministry, serving as a music director, Christian education director, and senior pastor in California and Canada. During his local church ministry, Dr. Blackaby became a college president, a missionary, and later an executive in Southern Baptist Convention life. In the early '90s he became one of North America's best-selling Christian authors, committed to helping people know and experience God. He and his wife, Marilynn, have five married children, all serving in Christian ministry. Dr. Blackaby is now serving as the president of Henry Blackaby Ministries.

KERRY L. SKINNER

Kerry L. Skinner has authored or co-authored many books with Dr. Henry Blackaby and Dr. Henry Brandt. He also has written curriculum for Prison Fellowship Ministry, which is used with thousands of inmates across North America. A graduate of Campbellsville College, where he is currently a trustee, and Southwestern Baptist Theological Seminary, Skinner has served in several churches as associate minister and minister of Christian education. Kerry Skinner currently serves as the executive vice president of Henry Blackaby Ministries. He and his wife, Elaine, have one son.

WITH GRATITUDE

We are thankful for the many people who have been
called by God and have lived a faithful life in
remaining accountable to Him. Their lives have been
a testimony to us and to the kingdom of God.

We especially thank Tony Stinson and Connie Yancey
for their contribution in the completing of this work.

Henry Blackaby Ministries
PO Box 161228
Atlanta, GA 30321
www.henryblackaby.com

BEFORE YOU BEGIN

Your study of *God's Purpose for Every Believer* can be a wonderful time of deepening your relationship with God. We pray that as you begin this encounter with God you will consider, notice, and remember several things:

1. *Consider* enlisting a prayer partner who will pray for you during the six-week study.

2. *Notice* there are testimonies provided along with each unit. These testimonies will help you see how other Christians, historical and modern-day, have understood and practiced *God's Purpose for Every Believer*.

3. *Notice* that the study is designed to guide you through five days of study each week. Please use the other two days to reflect on what God has spoken to you through the five days of guided study.

4.   *Notice* that every day an icon like this is placed somewhere in the text. When you see this icon, stop and take time to reflect, not only on the immediate paragraph where it appears, but sometimes on several paragraphs surrounding it. This reflection time may include: time for prayer, looking up other Scripture passages to discover their meaning, or simply taking time to apply what you are reading.

5. *Remember*, this is a time to encounter God, not simply to complete a study.

Small Group Or Individual Study?

The study can be done either way. However, if a group decides to go through the study together, there are a few guidelines provided for the leader in the Leader's Guide, found in the back of this book. Encourage individuals to complete each unit before you meet, then at your weekly group meeting give the group time to share what God is teaching them. Make sure you save time to pray together as God guides the group to know and experience that all are *Called and Accountable*!

Introduction

It is overwhelming to realize that the God of the universe, the only God and Creator of all that is, has chosen to call every believer into a very special relationship with Himself. This call and the relationship that follows are very personal and very real! The truth of this is found on almost every page of the Bible, in life after life, and verse after verse. It is central to the entire message of the Bible. It is, in fact, an expression of the very heart of God.

Even more amazing is the knowledge that it was God's choice to call people into such a personal relationship with Himself: *"He chose us in Him [Christ], before the foundation of the world, to be holy and blameless in His sight"* (Ephesians 1:4). Jesus expressed this will of the Father to His disciples this way: *"You did not choose Me, but I chose you. I appointed you that you should go out and produce fruit, and that your fruit should remain, so that whatever you ask the Father in My name, He will give you"* (John 15:16). This truth remains to this day, and includes each of us.

When this truth grips a person's heart, he or she is never the same again. Immediately there comes into that life a deep sense of meaning and purpose, and a sense of stewardship, or accountability, to God. So personal and real was this to David that he said to God,

My frame was not hidden from You,
When I was made in secret,
And skillfully wrought in the lowest parts of the earth.
Your eyes saw my substance, being yet unformed.
And in Your book they all were written,
The days fashioned for me,
When as yet there were none of them.

How precious also are Your thoughts to me, O God!
How great is the sum of them!
—Psalm 139:15–17

Jeremiah also was made aware of this when God informed him that:

Before I formed you in the womb I knew you;
Before you were born I sanctified you;
I ordained you a prophet to the nations.
—Jeremiah 1:5

God then unfolded to Jeremiah what this would mean to him, and the stewardship of this knowledge radically affected the rest of his life.

To give an even fuller picture of this truth, we must know the witness of the apostle Paul as he related what God had told him: "*God . . . from my mother's womb set me apart and called me by His grace*" (Galatians 1:15). Much of the Book of Acts is the record of what this call of God meant for Paul's life. Such love of God, Paul said, literally "constrained" him ("constrained" means to order all of the rest of his life). In this special relationship with God, he increasingly became convinced that, "*He died for all so that those who live should no longer live for themselves, but for the One who died for them and was raised*" (2 Corinthians 5:15). Paul went on later to express what this meant in his life in saying, "*But by God's grace I am what I am, and His grace toward me was not ineffective. However, I worked more than any of them, yet not I, but God's grace that was with me*" (1 Corinthians 15:10), thus expressing his enormous sense of accountability to God for such love toward him.

But this sense of call and accountability was not limited in the New Testament to just a few special people. **Every** believer is spoken of as the called of God, or the chosen of God, or ones set apart by God! (You may want to look up this fact in the following passages: Romans 1:6; 1 Corinthians 1:1–2; Ephesians 1:1–6, 18; Ephesians 4:1; 1 Thessalonians 1:4; 2 Thessalonians 1:11.)

As the Scriptures are our guide for both faith and practice, or daily living, this truth and its implications for each of our lives will guide us thoroughly in our relationship with God. This study will help us understand and respond to God in accountability. In this pursuit, we will look at:

1. **Why** does God call us?

2. **What** is a call?

3. **Who** are the called?

4. **How** am I called?

5. **When** am I called?

6. **How** do I live out this call?

CALLED & ACCOUNTABLE

UNIT 1

WHY DOES GOD CALL US?

UNIT 1
WHY DOES GOD CALL US?

ESSENTIAL TRUTH FOR THE WEEK

No one can adequately come to knowledge of God's truth, for themselves or for others, without a thorough commitment to the place and
authority of God's Word (the Scriptures). It is in the Scriptures that
God has chosen to reveal Himself and His will for our lives. As a
person approaches the Bible and opens its pages, he comes face to
face with the Author—God! The Holy Spirit is present to open the
mind and heart of the child of God to an immediate Word from God
for his or her life (John 14:17; John 16:13–15; 1 Corinthians
2:10–16). Without this commitment to encounter God in His Word,
one is left to human reasoning alone—something that will never lead
to God or an understanding of His Word. This entire study is based
on the assumption that the reader is committed to meet God in His
Word and respond to Him in this encounter.

Called & Accountable
R. G. LeTourneau

A Mechanic God Blessed

R. G. LeTourneau was one of the world's great inventors and industrialists. His company designed and built some of the world's largest heavy equipment. LeTourneau's inventions included the bulldozer, various kinds of scrapers and dredgers, portable cranes, logging equipment, and offshore drilling platforms. During World War II, LeTourneau built 70% of the heavy earthmoving equipment used by the Allies.

LeTourneau had not always been successful. He dropped out of school at age 14 and worked a variety of odd jobs for many years. At 28, he married his wife Evelyn, but their first child died in infancy. By age 31, he was deeply in debt due to the failure of his auto repair shop.

LeTourneau's setbacks caused him to turn back to the God he had met at 16 years of age. He said, "Lord, if you will forgive and help me, I'll do anything You want me to do from this day forward." When LeTourneau's pastor suggested that God needed godly businessmen, LeTourneau dedicated his life to using his business skills for the glory of God.

God began to bless LeTourneau's efforts, and he stuck to his commitment to be a businessman who was totally available to God. LeTourneau and his wife decided to give away 90% of their income and live on the remaining 10%, a commitment they kept for the rest of their lives. LeTourneau's factories held regular chapel services. He traveled all over the world sharing his testimony and the gospel. He started and funded missions efforts in Liberia, West Africa, and Peru.

LeTourneau died in 1969 at age 79, but his legacy lives on today through the school he and his wife founded in 1946, now known as LeTourneau University. The school continues to encourage its students to become Christian inventors and entrepreneurs and boasts more than 10,000 alumni serving the Lord in all 50 states and 55 countries worldwide.

LeTourneau often summed up his life with these words: "Friends, I'm just a sinner saved by grace. Just a mechanic that the Lord has blessed."

DAY 1
GOD'S WORD REVEALS GOD AND HIS WAYS

First, the entire Bible bears witness to the truth that God, from eternity, chose to work through His people to accomplish His eternal purposes in the world. He could have worked everything by Himself, just as He worked in creation, but He chose not to do it that way. Rather, the Bible tells how God called individuals into a special relationship with Himself at the very times He wanted to accomplish His purposes.

When God was about to destroy all living things from the earth because of sin, He called Noah to Himself, and through Noah preserved Noah, his family, and enough living creatures to begin to populate the earth again. When God wanted to establish saving faith for all mankind, He chose Abraham to be the one He would shape to be a sample of that faith to the end of time. When God was ready to deliver His chosen people from bondage in Egypt, He called Moses to Himself and sent Moses to be the one through whom He would accomplish this.

This became a revealed pattern throughout the entire Bible. It is still His way to this very hour. Throughout history, even since the writing of the New Testament, God has called ones He knew and could trust to be the instruments through which He would accomplish His eternal purposes, especially His purpose to redeem those who were lost.

GOD CALLED INDIVIDUALS INTO A SPECIAL RELATIONSHIP WITH HIMSELF AT THE VERY TIMES HE WANTED TO ACCOMPLISH HIS PURPOSES.

THROUGHOUT HISTORY, GOD HAS CALLED ONES HE KNEW AND COULD TRUST TO BE THE INSTRUMENTS THROUGH WHICH HE WOULD ACCOMPLISH HIS ETERNAL PURPOSES, ESPECIALLY HIS PURPOSE TO REDEEM THOSE WHO WERE LOST.

Similarly, this truth is revealed when God could not find a person through whom He could work to carry out His purpose to redeem. God would "call" someone to give the message of judgment and destruction. Ezekiel communicates such a moment when he records the heart of God saying,

> *"So I sought for a man among them who would make a wall, and stand in the gap before Me on behalf of the land, that I should not destroy it; but I found no one. Therefore I have poured out My indignation on them; I have consumed them with the fire of My wrath; and I have recompensed their deeds on their own heads," says the Lord GOD.*
> Ezekiel 22:30–31 (NKJV)

This is a most solemn truth, revealed by God—to us—so each of us will take seriously any invitation of God to be His instrument in saving others. This may be to bear witness to our family, our neighbors, or in some mission project involving personal and corporate evangelism. The eternal redemption of others may rest in our response to His invitation and call. And the Bible makes obvious the fact that He will hold us accountable for our response.

THE ETERNAL REDEMPTION OF OTHERS MAY REST IN OUR RESPONSE TO HIS INVITATION AND CALL. HE WILL HOLD US ACCOUNTABLE FOR OUR RESPONSE.

This same truth is seen in God's call on Ezekiel's life to be a "watchman" to God's people, for God. God did not want His people to suffer judgment, so He called Ezekiel and gave him an assignment to warn His people. God could have warned them Himself, but He chose instead to do it through His servant Ezekiel. Once Ezekiel had God's message for His people, he would be accountable for delivering it. Every Christian must read the nature of that serious accountability in Ezekiel 33:1–20 and apply it to their own lives today. This is why it is imperative that we believe the Scriptures. They reveal God and His ways, so that when God approaches us we will know that it is God, know how to respond to God, and know the serious nature of the consequences—for good, and for evil.

Read Ezekiel 33:1–20 to see the awesome message God assigned to Ezekiel. Then answer this question: What message has God entrusted to you for the benefit of the body of Christ?

I believe God has entrusted to
me the message with
my testimony to share with
others, I also think God has
put a heart for mission
in my life,

THE SCRIPTURES REVEAL GOD AND HIS WAYS, SO THAT WHEN GOD APPROACHES US WE WILL KNOW THAT IT IS GOD, KNOW HOW TO RESPOND TO GOD, AND KNOW THE SERIOUS NATURE OF THE CONSEQUENCES.

One of the most significant illustrations of this truth is found in the life of Mary, Jesus' mother. God's eternal purpose was to bring a Savior into the world, and through that Savior to bring His great salvation to every person. He found the one through whom He would choose to work—Mary, a quiet servant girl. An angel from God announced God's purpose through her. Then comes her amazing and wonderful response: "'Consider me the Lord's slave,' said Mary. 'May it be done to me according to your word.' Then the angel left her" (Luke 1:38). And God did what He said He would do! Impossible to man, but possible with God (Luke 1:37). Mary had a heart that was "perfect toward God" and God "proved Himself strong on her behalf" (2 Chronicles 16:9). This has been God's strategy from eternity, and still is—with each of us today.

God's Word consistently reveals this strategy of God, for our instruction in our day. The eternal destiny of multitudes hangs in the balance, as it always has, and God watches our response.

THOUGHT FOR THE DAY

GOD CHOOSES TO WORK THROUGH HIS PEOPLE TO ACCOMPLISH HIS ETERNAL PURPOSE.

Will your name be added to the list of the "faithful" found in Hebrews 11:39–40? Why?

My prayer is that God will place a seeking heart/serving so that one day I can be on that list.

Day 2
Called: Not for Time, But Eternity

In understanding the call of God in our lives, it is important to realize that God did not make us for time, but for eternity. We were created in His image (Genesis 1:26–27). This includes immortality (living for eternity). Jesus Himself declared constantly that the ones who believe in Him will have eternal life, and that we will reign with Him:

> **I grant you a kingdom, just as My Father granted one to Me, so that you may eat and drink at My table in My kingdom. And you will sit on thrones judging the 12 tribes of Israel.**
> Luke 22:29–30 (HCSB)

Paul also confirmed this by saying that when God saved us, *"He also raised us up with Him and seated us with Him in the heavens, in Christ Jesus"* (Ephesians 2:6); and that we were *"heirs of God and co-heirs with Christ"* (Romans 8:17). Thus, God's goal is not time, but eternity. This life, then, is to prepare us for eternity. This was God's purpose from before the foundation of the world.

Jesus further urged His disciples, *"Don't collect for your-selves treasures on earth . . . . But collect for yourselves treas-ures in heaven"* (Matthew 6:19–20).

Then God said, "Let Us make man in Our image, according to Our likeness." . . . So God created man in His own image; in the image of God He created him; male and female He created them.
Genesis 1:26–27

Make a list of the eternal investments that you have laid up in heaven. Compare that list with your earthly treasures.

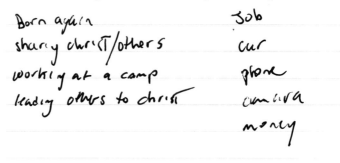

Born again — Job
sharing christ/others — car
working at a camp — phone
leading others to christ — camera
money

To Him, "time" was where eternal investments were made, but not where one should live without this understanding. Paul said,

> **Whatever you do, do it enthusiastically, as something done for the Lord and not for men, knowing that you will receive the reward of an inheritance from the Lord—you serve the Lord Christ.**
> COLOSSIANS 3:23-24 (HCSB)

Such incredible truth causes the Christian to pursue eternity, using "time" as God's gift in this pursuit. Therefore, every Christian will seek to use his or her time, this one life, to the maximum in the center of God's call. God's call is His invitation to invest in eternity by making our lives available to God when He calls and letting God work His eternal purposes through our lives, for God's glory!

THOUGHT FOR THE DAY

GOD'S PURPOSE IS FOR YOU TO <u>LIVE FOR ETERNITY</u>, NOT MERELY FOR "TIME."

Explain, as though you were talking with a friend, how a person would know that you are living for eternity.

Dear Friend,
    Time sometimes can fly by, and when you think about eternity I want to live each day of my life focusing on doing all I can do bring others to Christ. I haven't always had that best testimony but I hope others can see Christ shining through me.

DAY 3
CALL REQUIRES CHARACTER

GOD IS SEEKING TO DEVELOP THE CHARACTER OF HIS SON JESUS IN EACH OF US. THIS IS HIS ETERNAL PURPOSE. HE WOULD DO THROUGH OUR LIVES WHAT HE WAS ABLE TO DO THROUGH HIS SON.

God's goal for each believer is *"to be conformed to the image of His Son"* (Romans 8:29).

That is, God is seeking to develop the character of His Son Jesus in each of us. This is His eternal purpose. He would do through our lives what He was able to do through His Son. Because of the character of His Son (sinlessness), God was able to do His will completely. Notice this Scripture:

> *During His earthly life, He offered prayers and appeals, with loud cries and tears, to the One who was able to save Him from death, and He was heard because of His reverence. Though a Son, He learned obedience through what He suffered. After He was perfected, He became the source of eternal salvation to all who obey Him.*
> HEBREWS 5:7–9 (HCSB)

Eternal salvation would come to all who obey Him, and eternal salvation would come through all of His children when they made their lives as available to God as His Son was available to Him. His salvation would come to the ends of the earth, to every person, developing character through those He would call, then shape for His purposes, and then work through them according to His eternal purposes.

This is what Jesus prayed:

> *Sanctify them by the truth; Your word is truth. Just as*
> *You sent Me into the world, I also have sent them into*
> *the world. I sanctify Myself for them, so they also*
> *may be sanctified by the truth.*
>
> JOHN 17:17–19 (HCSB)

He wanted His disciples to be "set apart for God," as He was set apart for God. This was to be "into the world" where God was not willing that any perish, but that all come to repentance! This is God's eternal purpose for each of our lives also, in this our day. This is a very serious and eternal purpose of God, to be worked out in our lives, as it was in Jesus' life.

So God is seeking to develop in us the character of His Son. It is important at this time in our study to place clearly before us this key passage in Romans:

> *We know that all things work together for the good of*
> *those who love God; those who are called according*
> *to His purpose. For those He foreknew He also pre-*
> *destined to be conformed to the image of His Son, so*
> *that He would be the firstborn among many brothers.*
> *And those He predestined, He also called; and those*
> *He called, He also justified; and those He justified,*
> *He also glorified.*
>
> ROMANS 8:28–30 (HCSB)

This truth carries with it so much of the "why" of our being called of God. Such character is developed in the crucible of a relationship with Him in our world as He works out in our life His eternal plan of redemption. He calls us into a relationship with Himself, so that in the relationship we can come to know Him and experience His working in us and through us. In that relationship, and only there, does He develop character in us in preparation for an eternity with Him. This may sound to you at this time in our study very "heavy." It is—but it is the heart of the Christian's life!

What is the major character trait that God developed in:
Abraham

> Faith, Trust

Moses

> Leader

Jeremiah

> Perseverance

David

> Righteous, humble, warrior

Paul

> Faithful, courages

You

> Compasion

This pattern of God, taking the responsibility for developing character in the ones He called for His purposes, is seen in such persons as Abraham, Moses, Jeremiah, David, the disciples, and Paul. This pattern continued all through history. Those God used mightily would themselves, in their biographies, bear witness to this significant character-building activity of God in their lives.

THOUGHT FOR THE DAY

CHARACTER IS DEVELOPED IN THE CRUCIBLE OF A RELATIONSHIP WITH GOD WHILE LIVING IN THE REALITY OF THIS WORLD.

What character is God developing in your life?

I believe he is Developing the character of a man with a heart to seek him more and to share the gospel with others.

DAY 4
CONFORMED TO THE IMAGE OF CHRIST

The entire process of developing Christlike character in every believer begins when God calls us to Himself in a relationship of love. He first redeems us from our sin, forgiving us and cleansing us and setting us apart for Himself. He places His Son in us (Colossians 1:27–29), and His Son begins to live out His life in each believer (Galatians 2:20), until each believer is "perfect [i.e., complete] in Christ" (Colossians 1:28). Paul said, *"until Christ is formed in you"* (Galatians

THE PROCESS OF DEVELOPING CHRISTLIKE CHARACTER IN EVERY BELIEVER BEGINS WHEN GOD CALLS US TO HIMSELF IN A RELATIONSHIP OF LOVE.

4:19), he would labor with God tirelessly on their behalf.

Look up and read Colossians 1:27–29; Galatians 2:20; Colossians 1:28; and Galatians 4:19. Then write how God called you into a relationship with Him.

I believe God called me into a relationship with him by allowing the things I treasured most in my life like going out with my x-girlfriend

GOD IS NOT WILLING THAT ANY SHOULD PERISH, IN ANY GENERATION OR IN ANY PART OF THE WORLD.

The relationship of love that God initiates in the believer continues throughout the rest of life. God develops us, equips us, and takes us on mission with Himself into our world. God is not willing that any should perish, in any generation or in any part of the world.

Throughout the Bible there are many persons God called to Himself. We could study any one of these persons and see this eternal purpose of God unfolding. But we will only take one example—the disciples Jesus "called to Himself." As Jesus called His disciples, He said, "Follow Me!" And they immediately left all and followed Him.

First, Jesus knew that each had been given to Him by the Father. At the close of His life, as He prayed in the Garden of Gethsemane, He affirmed,

I have revealed Your name to the men You gave Me from the world. They were Yours, You gave them to Me, and they have kept Your word. Now they know that all things You have given to Me are from You, because the words that You gave to Me, I have given to them. They have received them and have known for certain that I came from You. They have believed that You sent Me.

JOHN 17:6–8 (HCSB)

Second, Jesus knew absolutely that it was His assignment from the Father to prepare these men for the Father's eternal purpose. That purpose was to take the Good News of His great salvation to the ends of the earth. This purpose would happen after His assignment was completed to reconcile the world to God through the Cross, the Resurrection, and the Ascension.

For the entire three and one-half years of Jesus' ministry this is what He did. He took the disciples with Him as He taught, preached, and healed. He revealed to them the Father, and the Father's purposes—and the disciples believed. When Jesus returned to the Father, He sent the disciples into the world, in the same way the Father had sent Him into the world (John 17:18; 20:21). The "keys of the Kingdom of Heaven" were in their hands (Matthew 16:19). They would be working with the Father and the Son, in the power of the Holy Spirit, to fulfill the Father's purpose to redeem a lost world to Himself.

This was the Father's way, and is still the Father's way, in each of our lives who believe in His Son, Jesus Christ. The

Just as You sent Me into the world, I also have sent them into the world.
JOHN 17:18

Jesus said to them again, "Peace to you! Just as the Father has sent Me, I also send you."
JOHN 20:21

Father calls us to His Son and gives us to Him. Jesus is still entrusted with receiving us from the Father and giving us eternal life (John 17:2–3). He continues teaching and guiding each believer, molding them as the Father has instructed Him until each knows the Father and responds to Him. Just as the early disciples experienced a relationship with Him, the more one responds, the more God uses that individual to go with Him and His Risen Son on a redemptive mission to the ends of the earth. As the disciples obeyed the Lord in this relationship of love, God turned their world upside down (Acts 17:6). All through history, God has continued to do this, and desires once again in our generation to do this same work of love.

THOUGHT FOR THE DAY

REMEMBER THAT GOD, WHO REVEALS HIS PURPOSES TO WORK THROUGH THOSE HE CALLS, IS DOING THIS IN YOUR LIFE ALSO. YOU HAVE BEEN GIVEN TO HIS SON, AND HIS SON KNOWS WHAT THE FATHER HAS IN MIND FOR YOUR LIFE—IN YOUR WORLD.

Write a few examples of how you would know your life is being conformed to the image of Christ.

- If co-workers started asking why I am the way I am
- If fellow followers come to the scene.

DAY 5
BECAUSE HE LOVES US . . .

With this pattern from the Scriptures clearly before us, we can now ask this life-changing question again: "Why does God call us?" But we need to be careful when we ask God this question! To ask God a question is a very serious matter. For God will answer us, and when He does we are fully accountable for our response to Him. To sin in ignorance is one thing! But to sin with knowledge is a much more serious thing (Hebrews 10:26–31).

Read Hebrews 10:26–31 now, and consider the serious way God treats the knowledge of truth.

In the mind and heart of God so much is at stake! His call to us is not merely so we can go to heaven when we die. There is so much more involved than that. Look at how God develops His purpose in those He calls:

1. God saves us so we can come to know and experience Him fully! To "know" Him is to love Him. And to love Him is to trust and obey Him.

2. Jesus said that the one who loves Him will obey Him. And the one who obeys Him will be loved by the Father and the Son and that He will reveal Himself to him. The Father, the Son, and the Holy Spirit would all take up permanent residence in him (John 14:21, 23; 14:15–18).

TO ASK GOD A QUESTION IS A VERY SERIOUS MATTER. FOR GOD WILL ANSWER US, AND WHEN HE DOES WE ARE FULLY ACCOUNTABLE FOR OUR RESPONSE TO HIM.

TO SIN IN IGNORANCE IS ONE THING! BUT TO SIN WITH KNOWLEDGE IS A MUCH MORE SERIOUS THING.

Read John 14:21, 23, 14:15–18 now. Are there any ways in which you have not kept God's commandments? If so, what areas of your life must change?

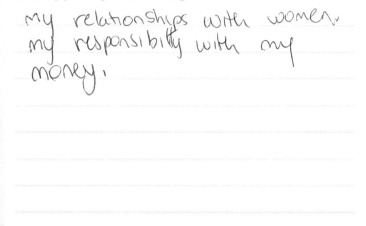

My relationships with women. my responsibity with my money.

3. With the Father, the Son, and the Holy Spirit's presence within, we would be changed into the likeness of the Lord Jesus (2 Corinthians 3:16–18).

4. With the presence of God fully within (Ephesians 3:16–21), we would, personally and within the corporate life of God's people, experience Him doing *"above and beyond all that we ask or think—according to the power that works in you"* (v. 20), and He would receive glory *"in the church and in Christ Jesus to all generations, forever and ever"* (v. 21).

5. This transformation would call us to be on mission with Him in our world, and this would affect eternity.

6. This would be according to His eternal plan, worked out in each one who believes Him, in every generation.

Once we know this, how we respond to Him will reveal what we believe about Him.

We do love Him! We do have an inner desire, created by God, to serve Him with all our hearts! And now God waits for our response—to Him!

THOUGHT FOR THE DAY

HE CHOSE US BECAUSE HE LOVED US! NOW, IN THIS LOVE, HE ASKS THAT WE LOVE HIM WITH ALL OUR HEARTS, MINDS, SOULS, AND STRENGTH!

How would you answer the question, "Why did God call you?"

I believe God called me because I am very approachable and easy to talk to. I believe that he is going to use me to reach people by becoming their friends.

CALLED & ACCOUNTABLE
COUNT NICHOLAS ZINZENDORF

"ALL THIS I DID FOR THEE, WHAT HAST THOU DONE FOR ME?"

Zinzendorf was born in 1700 in Dresden, Germany, into one of the noblest families of Europe.

As a young adult, Nicholas visited an art museum in Düsseldorf, Germany, where he saw the painting by Domenico Feti titled, "Ecce Homo" (Behold the Man). The painting depicted the risen Christ with the legend, "All this I did for thee, what hast thou done for Me?" The face of Christ in the painting never left his heart, and Christ's love became the compelling force of his life.

Zinzendorf's love for his Savior was expressed in his love for other believers, especially through a small group of approximately 300 Moravians whom he allowed to establish a church on his estate at Herrnhut in 1722. He helped the Moravians develop a deep passion for their Savior and helped them to live out Christ's command to love one another.

Zinzendorf's love for Christ was also expressed through his life of prayer. He spent countless hours in communion with his Savior and sought to lead others to commit to a life of prayer. His example led the Moravian believers to begin a powerful prayer movement they called "hourly intercession." They prayed in shifts, twenty-four hours a day, seven days a week, for the work of Christ around the world. This "hourly intercession" went on uninterrupted for over one hundred years!

Zinzendorf's passion for Jesus was also manifested in his desire to reach those who did not know his Savior. By 1752, the Moravian Church at Herrnhut had sent out more missionaries than the whole Protestant church had done in 200 years. Before long they had three members on the mission field for every one at their church in Herrnhut. All this was accomplished by men and women with little formal and theological education, but with a burning passion for their Savior, Jesus Christ.

Zinzendorf's life was a labor of love for his Savior, who had done so much for him and a lost and dying world.

CALLED & ACCOUNTABLE

UNIT 2
WHAT IS A CALL?

Unit 2
What Is a Call?

Essential Truth for the Week

One must believe that God really does speak to us in this matter of His call. From Genesis through Revelation, no truth stands out any clearer than that God "speaks" to His people. They always know that it is God, they know what He is saying, and they know how they are to respond. In other words, this is not all just an academic exercise or a merely "theological truth." It is a real relationship with God, and He really does call each of us to Himself for His eternal purposes. This is very foundational!

Called & Accountable
Cheryl Wolfinger

"No Money, No Plan, Just God's Call on My Life."

"Me, start an international sports ministry? I am too young, too inexperienced, and have no idea how to even begin!"

Cheryl Wolfinger, age 27, did know something about basketball. From the first grade, Cheryl knew that she wanted to be a basketball player. Playing time in a European basketball league followed her successful high school and college career. Through her involvement with the Fellowship of Christian Athletes (FCA), Cheryl had also been able to share with other athletes her love for Jesus Christ.

However, when a missionary shared with Cheryl the need to mobilize and network Christian athletes to do sports evangelism internationally, Cheryl's reaction was, "Great idea, God, but You have got the wrong person!" Yet, as she looked at how God had been working in her life, she realized that He had been preparing her for just such an assignment. So with no money and no plan, just God's call on her life, Cheryl began the International Sports Federation (ISF) in April 1993.

During her first sports mission trip to Madagascar in 1993, God showed Cheryl how His plan and her obedience could touch a lost world:

After playing the national team, I gave one of the girls a Bible in her own language and told her what Jesus meant to me. As I walked away I realized that she listened to me, not because I could preach, or sing, or do the typical mission activities, but because I could dribble a basketball. No matter how war-torn or impoverished the country, people will play. There are countries where it is illegal to evangelize, but nowhere is it illegal to carry a basketball and use it to build a relationship.

Since 1993, over 4,000 ISF volunteers have completed over 500 projects in 70 countries. Thousands of lives have been touched because a basketball player said "Yes" to God's call on her life.

*To find out how God could use your athletic skills to make a difference in a lost world, visit www.teamisf.com.

DAY 1
A CALL TO RELATIONSHIP

From the very beginning, in the Garden of Eden, we see God bringing Adam into being and "calling" him to Himself. It was preeminently a call to a love relationship with God. God created him in His love. He instructed Adam (and later, Eve) to partner with Him by naming the animals and by having dominion over all God had created (Genesis 1:28). God continued to give Adam and Eve instructions about the stewardship and accountability of their assignments. The character of God's perfect creation is found in the repetitive words, "God spoke! And it was so! And it was good!"

This was supremely true about God's relationship of love with Adam and Eve. This is always true with God when He brings any person into His world!

But sin entered into the lives of Adam and Eve, and the loving relationship with God was broken. One weeps just in reading again the pitiful picture of Adam and Eve hiding themselves from the Presence of God (Genesis 3:8). And then the heartcry of God, "Adam, where are you?" (Genesis 3:9–10). Adam and Eve were now afraid of God. What a change in relationship!

The rest of the Bible is the story of God pursuing this relationship of love with His children. In every generation God called His people to return to a love relationship with Him. The Bible is the story of God's redemptive love providing everyone who will believe Him a way back to His love.

Then the LORD God called to Adam and said to him, "Where are you?"
GENESIS 3:9

THE BIBLE IS THE STORY OF GOD'S REDEMPTIVE LOVE PROVIDING EVERYONE WHO WILL BELIEVE HIM A WAY BACK TO HIS LOVE.

God provided salvation through His Son, so that His eternal purpose of love could be restored.

But we too often think of this salvation as simply providing a way for us to go to heaven when we die. This is certainly a vital part of God's great salvation, for as we have noted, God did not create us for time, but for **eternity**! But it will be important at this point in our study to keep in mind Jesus' definition of "eternal life":

This is eternal life: that they may know You, the only true God, and the One You have sent—Jesus Christ.

JOHN 17:3 (HCSB)

The Amplified Bible will help us to understand this definition more intimately. John 17:3 and Philippians 3:10 define eternal life clearly:

And this is eternal life: [it means] to know (to perceive, recognize, become acquainted with and understand) You, the only true and real God, and [likewise] to know Him, Jesus [as the] Christ, the Anointed One, the Messiah, Whom You have sent.

JOHN 17:3 (AMPLIFIED)

[For my determined purpose is] that I may know Him—that I may progressively become more deeply and intimately acquainted with Him, perceiving and recognizing and understanding [the wonders of His Person] more strongly and more clearly. And that I

> *may in that same way come to know the power out-flowing from His resurrection [which it exerts over believers]; and that I may so share His sufferings as to be continually transformed [in spirit into His likeness even] to His death.*
>
> PHILIPPIANS 3:10 (AMPLIFIED)

Thus God's call is to His great salvation, provided in His Son, and provided as an incredible expression of His eternal love for each of us. You catch the enormous nature of this relationship as the apostle Paul bears witness to his new "life **in Christ**." This is pure relationship. Hear a few of Paul's attempts to describe his new life "in Christ":

1. *"For to me, living is Christ, and dying is gain."* (Philippians 1:21, HCSB)

2. *"I have been crucified with Christ; and I no longer live, but Christ lives in me. The life I now live in the flesh, I live by faith in the Son of God, who loved me and gave Himself for me."* (Galatians 2:19–20, HCSB)

3. *"I am able to do all things through Him who strengthens me."* (Philippians 4:13, HCSB)

4. *"But by God's grace I am what I am, and His grace toward me was not ineffective. However, I worked more than any of them, yet not I, but God's grace that was with me."* (1 Corinthians 15:10, HCSB)

Paul's letters are full of such expressions of love to his Lord. He speaks out of his personal experience when he urges every believer to *"be filled with the Spirit"* (Ephesians 5:18) and to be *"filled with all the fullness of God"* (Ephesians 3:19).

Make a list of Scriptures that are favorites to you that describe your new life in Christ.

_____

_____

_____

_____

_____

_____

_____

This is the testimony of all the great servants of God, both in Scripture and in history. They always tell of the overwhelming relationship of love that took place when they were called of God.

THOUGHT FOR THE DAY

THIS "CALL" OF GOD TO EVERY BELIEVER IS TO AN INTIMATE AND LIFE-GIVING RELATIONSHIP WITH GOD, WHICH IS TOTALLY LIFE-TRANSFORMING AND ULTIMATELY WORLD-CHANGING WITH GOD.

Describe how your life has been transformed since you came into an intimate relationship with Christ.

_____

_____

_____

_____

_____

_____

_____

_____

_____

_____

_____

DAY 2
THE CALL IS REDEMPTIVE

There is another aspect of this relationship and calling, one that is so often overlooked or neglected. That is, that this relationship is always **redemptive**! The call to salvation is at the same time a call to be redemptively on mission with God in our world. The moment any person is brought into a relationship with God, they experience the heart of God and the mind of God and the eternal purposes of God. All that is on the heart of the Son of God, who now dwells within us, now increasingly becomes a part of our heart as well. And the

THE CALL TO SALVATION IS AT THE SAME TIME A CALL TO BE REDEMPTIVELY ON MISSION WITH GOD IN OUR WORLD.

Spirit, who also now dwells within, shares His life with us as well, and this always involves the will of the Father (John 16:13–15). It is impossible to live intimately with God and not be *"transformed into the same image from glory to glory; this is from the Lord who is the Spirit"* (2 Corinthians 3:18).

How do you sense you are on mission with God?

This will essentially bring into us a burden that is the heart of God—that God is *"not willing that any should perish but that all should come to repentance"* (2 Peter 3:9, NKJV). God, who sent His only Son into the world that we through Him might be saved (John 3:16), will also send us into the world that others, through us, might be saved (by our witness to His great salvation).

This truth, again, is seen throughout the entire Bible, and all those mightily used throughout history bear witness to the reality of this. From the moment of salvation there comes over the new believer a deep sense of being on mission with the Lord in their world. Some indicate that at salvation they sensed a call to mission, evangelism, and witness. This is normal for every new believer.

FROM THE MOMENT OF SALVATION THERE COMES OVER THE NEW BELIEVER A DEEP SENSE OF BEING ON MISSION WITH THE LORD IN THEIR WORLD.

In Philippians 2:3–11, Paul urged the believers in the church at Philippi to "*make your own attitude that of Christ Jesus*" (vs. 5) and then listed what this would mean specifically. He expected Christ to be formed in them, so he urged them to let Him do so. Then he added,

> **Work out your own salvation with fear and trembling. For it is God who is working among you both the willing and the working for His good purpose.**
>
> PHILIPPIANS 2:12–13 (HCSB)

What he meant was that each believer must let the full implications of their salvation work out into every area of life. Each must respond to Him as Lord over all of life, for it is now He who will be working in the life of the believer, causing them to want to do His will, and then working in their life to enable them to do it. What an exciting possibility for every believer!

Let me illustrate this process in one life I had the privilege to touch, as his pastor.

Gerry Taillon came from a Roman Catholic background. He was a university student in the city in Canada where I pastored. A friend of Gerry's, who had become a Christian and was now a member of our church, helped Gerry become a Christian. From the beginning of his Christian life, Gerry lived with a deep inner sense of a call to be on mission with his Savior. Within a few weeks he came to the church body weeping, saying, "God wants me to be fully available to Him. Today I release my life to do anything that needs to be done. Is there some need that I can meet?"

That week I had received an urgent call from the pastor of a First Nations church in Cochin, Saskatchewan, expressing a need for a Sunday School teacher. (First Nations is the preferred name for Canadian native peoples.) Gerry eagerly agreed to drive the 120 miles one way each Sunday. He did this for several years, taking other students to help him. Then the old pastor's health broke, and he had to return to the U.S.

The First Nations congregation asked Gerry to be their pastor. His servant heart responded, and for several years he pastored them. He and his wife, Connie, completed university, then studied at Golden Gate Baptist Theological Seminary. While they were there, another urgent call came for someone with a Roman Catholic and French background to anchor our work in Quebec, a French Catholic province. Again Gerry was totally available to God and responded.

Gerry and Connie and their three children then served faithfully in Montreal, Quebec, giving direction to all our Southern Baptist work in this needy province. When the Canadian Convention of Southern Baptists was looking for a new executive director of their convention, they looked to Gerry. He is now serving in that role with a God-given heart for taking the gospel to every person in Canada. The convention has about 163 churches and missions in Canada, and under Gerry's guidance they now have a heart to establish 1,000 new churches by the year 2020.

Throughout the Bible and throughout history, those mightily used of God have had this same pattern in their lives. My own Christian life began with a deep sense that God had something in mind when He saved me (John 15:16).

> *You did not choose Me, but I chose you. I appointed you that you should go out and produce fruit, and that your fruit should remain, so that whatever you ask the Father in My name, He will give you.*
>
> JOHN 15:16 (HCSB)

Anything that God presented to me, I responded to Him as His servant. I began by leading youth. As I led the youth I watched for anything God would desire to do through my life. Then a church asked if I would be their music/education director. It never crossed my mind not to respond, for I knew that the call to salvation was at the same time the call to serve with God in my world.

Two years later, that same church asked if I would be their pastor. I did so and served for five years. Later some churches asked if I would be their director of missions. I agreed and served for six years. Then the Home Mission Board [later named the North American Mission Board] asked if I would guide our convention toward prayer and spiritual awakening. I did that with them as well as with the International Mission Board and LifeWay Christian Resources until April of 2000.

THOUGHT FOR THE DAY

THERE IS NOTHING MORE AWESOME TO THE NEW BELIEVER THAN TO SENSE THAT THE GOD OF THE UNIVERSE HAS CALLED THEM TO BE ON MISSION WITH HIM IN THEIR WORLD. STAND BEFORE GOD, AND TREMBLE!

How has God worked out His salvation in you?

How has God redeemed your life to put you in a position to be on mission with Him?

_____

_____

_____

_____

_____

_____

_____

_____

_____

_____

_____

Day 3
A Call to Mission

Every Christian is called of God to salvation, and in that same call is the call to be on mission with God in our world. This is what it means to be called. God is seeking to bring a lost world back to Himself. He loves every person. He is not willing that any should perish. He has always been working in our world to seek and to save those who are lost. That is what He was doing when He called you! Those He saves, He involves as fellow workers with Himself in His eternal purpose to save a lost world.

But to every sincere leader in every succeeding generation, Paul adds significantly, *"Look, now is the acceptable time; look, now is the day of salvation"* (2 Corinthians 6:2). In other words, the moment of their call was the moment God would be at work to redeem their world. It would be God's strategic moment of favor toward the people to whom the gospel would be preached. Paul knew this in real experience, for he was living as a "worker with God." Wherever Paul was at work, he was not only invited to "join God" but was given the enabling grace of God to be used of God to bring multitudes to salvation, just as God had planned to do.

This is strategically important for every believer to understand. For each believer, *"now is the acceptable time [time of God's favor] . . . now is the day of salvation"* (2 Corinthians 6:2). This moment is God's moment for each person, the time for God to work through them.

God has placed you in this strategic moment to be of help to His people. How has God chosen to use your life among His people?

I see this unfolding day after day in the life of CEOs in corporate America. I have the wonderful privilege of "working" with more than 120 of these strategic men and women, placed in the corporate world of the nation by God for such a time as this! God is touching their minds and hearts deeply. They have an inner sense that God not only is at work in them and around them, but that God clearly wants greater access to work His Kingdom purposes through them. They are "seeking the Lord with all their hearts" as God said He would cause them to do. And they are readying their lives, their marriages, their homes, and their business lives to be available to God in a maximum way. And month after month we hear how God is doing exactly this for His purposes in our day.

I am hearing this same pattern of God's activity in teenagers in their schools, in college students on their campuses, and in so many women who believe that God is about to work toward a great revival in the nation through women wholly available to God. I believe this may be a vital part of God's strategy for redeeming our world in our day.

There is a sudden and extensive move of God, causing every believer to sense that their life is indeed "on mission with God" at this time.

THOUGHT FOR THE DAY

GOD IS TRULY ON MISSION WITH HIS PEOPLE IN OUR DAY. THERE IS NO SENSE THAT ONLY A FEW ARE CALLED! ALL ARE CALLED, AND EACH CHRISTIAN IS URGED TO *"WALK WORTHY OF THE CALLING"* (EPHESIANS 4:1–3).

What distinctive opportunity to serve God has He brought to your life?

_____

_____

_____

_____

_____

_____

_____

_____

_____

_____

DAY 4
GOD INITIATES THE CALL

In this entire process, God takes the initiative to come to His people and to let them know what He is doing or about to do. He came to Noah at the moment He was about to judge the world by a flood. Unless God had come to him, Noah could not have known what was about to happen. But Noah did know because God wanted to accomplish His purpose through Noah. So God gave Noah an assignment, and Noah responded as a co-worker with God.

When God was about to free several million of His people from slavery in Egypt, He took the initiative to come to

Moses and let Moses know what He was about to do. This revelation was God's invitation for Moses to work with Him to accomplish His purposes for His people. God came this way to each of the prophets.

To the disciples Jesus said, *"You did not choose Me, but I chose you. I appointed you that you should go out and produce fruit, and that your fruit should remain, so that whatever you ask the Father in My name, He will give you."* (John 15:16). To the apostle Paul and to God's people throughout history, this pattern is found every time He is about to do a great work in our world, and it is still true today! It is true right now for your life also!

This call of God will always involve some kind of major adjustment in your life to be the person God can use to accomplish His purposes. Moses had to leave herding sheep. David could not keep doing what he was doing and be king at the same time. The disciples of Jesus could no longer continue fishing and go with Jesus at the same time. In our day, when lawyers, doctors, schoolteachers, truck drivers, salespeople, nurses, or bankers become Christians, they respond to Christ as Lord over all of their lives, so He can accomplish His plans through His people.

What major adjustment is God making in your life so that you can bear maximum fruit?

_____

_____

_____

_____

_____

_____

_____

_____

_____

God may leave Christians in their present vocation or professional position. However, it will not be "business as usual," or business as the world around them would have it. They will thoroughly realize that they have been "bought with a price," and therefore they are, at all times and in all places, to make sure that they glorify God in their bodies and in their souls which are His (1 Corinthians 6:19–20). Since God dwells fully within them, every place they put their feet is holy ground, for God is present in them. That makes their workplace a place where God can accomplish His eternal purposes through them, right there! The classroom becomes a "workplace for God" for one called to be a teacher. The workshop is God's place of evangelism for a car mechanic. The doctor's office or surgery suite becomes God's workplace for a medical doctor or nurse. The lawyer's office or courtroom for the lawyer or judge, and the halls of government for the congressman or mayor or political official, all become God's workplace. But the choice, the arena of activity God chooses for each believer, is entirely up to God. Someone has effectively said, "The command of God is to go! We will have to get His permission to stay home!" This is true.

THE ARENA OF ACTIVITY GOD CHOOSES FOR EACH BELIEVER IS ENTIRELY UP TO GOD.

One of the greatest developments today is the tremendous number of missions volunteers who are leaving all and following Jesus—across America and around the world. Teachers are going into China so that our Lord can reach Chinese people through them. Businesspeople are making their lives available through their business connections around the world so Christ can bring lost persons to Himself who would not hear any other way. Tens of thousands of volunteers are going around the world each year with a deep sense of being on mission with their Lord. What a difference this is making in our generation!

A young woman doctor recently gave the first years of her practice to go and work in Yemen while her husband served as a teacher in the school. They will never be the same again, and people have heard the gospel who would not otherwise have heard. The call to salvation is a call to go on mission with our Lord in our world.

But none have gone without major adjustments in their lives. Some had to give up their successful medical or legal practice; others had to leave aging parents; others had to risk their health and their children; still others had to learn new languages and adapt to strange customs and cultures. But God has chosen to reach a lost world through those He calls to become His children through faith in His Son. Such love is what God counts on to move us to go with Him into our lost world.

WHATEVER GOD INITIATES IN THE BELIEVER'S LIFE, GOD EXPECTS AN IMMEDIATE, "YES, LORD!" WHEN BELIEVERS ARE AVAILABLE TO GOD, GOD CAN AND WILL COMPLETE HIS WORK THROUGH THEM
(JOHN 12:24–26).

To what mission is God calling you?

_____

_____

_____

_____

_____

_____

_____

DAY 5
A CALL TO OBEDIENCE

If every believer were to think carefully about their present relationship with God, they would realize that their greatest challenge is not that they do not know the will of God, but rather that they *do* know His will but have not been willing to be obedient to Him! Neither God nor history waits on the believer's response to God's call and claim on their life.

FOR MANY, THE GREATEST CHALLENGE IS NOT THAT THEY DO NOT KNOW THE WILL OF GOD, BUT RATHER THAT THEY *DO* KNOW HIS WILL BUT HAVE NOT BEEN WILLING TO BE OBEDIENT TO HIM!

God's call requires only one response from every believer—**obedience**! Once you, as a child of God, know the initiative of God in your life, you must immediately without resistance or discussion respond obediently to all God is directing. Only then will you experience God's working mightily through your life.

This was true in the life of Hudson Taylor. He was training as a medical doctor. When God made it unmistakably clear that He wanted to reach the peoples of inland China with the gospel through Taylor's life, obedience was all that was left for him. He was obedient, and God did reach hundreds of thousands, even millions, of precious Chinese people through Hudson Taylor's life and those God would bring alongside of him to preach, teach, and heal in China.

Further, a call from God always involves the person in the corporate life of the people of God. Even God's call to Abram involved all the people of God who would follow Abram. God's call to Moses directly involved God's purposes in the life of Israel, His people. God's calls to Joshua, or the judges, or Samuel, or David, or the prophets, or the disciples, or Paul—all brought them into the midst of what God had purposed to do through their lives as His people.

What task has God assigned to you in your local church?

In the New Testament, the redemptive work of God was to be through the life of His people functioning together in local churches. Through these churches, God would take His great salvation to the ends of the earth, even to "every person." Every believer should anticipate that God will involve them dynamically in their local church. God will then, as He did in the New Testament, involve each church in the life of sister churches that He has established in His Kingdom. This will involve each church with churches of other denominations, as well.

The call of God is always a call to the whole world through all of His people, everywhere!

THOUGHT FOR THE DAY

OBEDIENCE IS ALWAYS THE KEY TO EXPERIENCING A LIFE ON MISSION WITH GOD IN OUR WORLD!

Is there any area of your life in which God is calling for obedience but you have not yet responded? If so, explain.

CALLED & ACCOUNTABLE
MATT AND DONNA

WHY DON'T YOU GO?

Matt and Donna were "good Christians." Raised by parents who loved Jesus, both received Christ as their Savior at an early age. Their churches helped them to grow in their faith. They met while earning college degrees in computer science, and eventually decided that God wanted them to spend the rest of their lives together.

Following marriage, Matt and Donna pursued career goals and began to have a family. With four kids and an advancing career, Matt and Donna found themselves in the middle of the suburban American lifestyle.

During a missions conference at their church, God began to speak to both of them. They heard about the 1.7 billion people living in the world who have little to no opportunity to hear about Jesus Christ. They discovered that their denomination of 16 million members had only 5,000 international missionaries. Donna wondered, "With so many people needing the gospel and so few missionaries, why aren't more people willing to go?" God responded loud and clear to Donna: "Why don't you go?"

It had never occurred to Matt that God would want him to go. Although heavily involved in church, he had never considered how God wanted them involved in His plan to reach the world. Matt was focused on the corporate ladder. Along with church, he was busy building their retirement funds, drawing up plans to expand their home, choosing a new Sport Utility Vehicle, and sending their kids to the best schools possible. Missions was not in the formula for their success. But suddenly God revealed to Matt that there were people all around the world who were more important than their plans and their stuff.

Matt and Donna told God, "We are willing to go!" When they made their lives available to God, they discovered that there was a great need on the mission field for those with experience in computer science. Today, they are serving in East Asia as missionaries, using their administrative and technical abilities to share Jesus Christ with those who have never heard.

CALLED & ACCOUNTABLE

UNIT 3
WHO ARE THE CALLED?

Unit 3
Who Are the Called?

Essential Truth for the Week

Every believer is called to "*walk worthy of the calling you have received*" (Ephesians 4:1–3).

Ephesians 4:1—*I, therefore, the prisoner in the Lord, urge you to walk worthy of the calling you have received,*

Ephesians 4:2—*with all humility and gentleness, with patience, accepting one another in love,*

Ephesians 4:3—*diligently keeping the unity of the Spirit with the peace that binds us.*

CALLED & ACCOUNTABLE
CHARLES BEATY

"WE ARE NOT PROMISED TOMORROW"

"Whom shall we send and who will go for us?" Charles and Christy Beaty heard God's call to them in 1994, and their answer was, "Here am I, send me." One year later, the Beatys found themselves in northern Africa as career missionaries with the International Mission Board.

They had not grown up dreaming of becoming missionaries. Charles and Christy were focused on their insurance business, settling down in Kansas City, Kansas, and raising a family. Yet they responded to God's call, believing that there were people living with little or no access to the Gospel who needed to hear the message that Jesus Christ is Lord.

After serving for two years in Northern Africa, Charles and Christy received some devastating news. Charles, 30, had adenocarcinoma of the lung, a very serious form of lung cancer. Charles battled for several years, but when he was only 34, the doctors told him that he would be dead in just a few months.

Charles decided to spend the final months of his life mobilizing Christians to reach a lost and dying world for Jesus Christ. His words challenge us to respond now to God's call: *Is the Lord calling you today to go, to go to the people who have no voice? My challenge to you is go, and don't wait, because we are not promised tomorrow."*

Asked how he wanted to be remembered, Charles said, *"I want them to think of the peoples of North Africa who will die and go into eternity hopeless without Christ. I want them to think, 'I'm going to go and live out my life for Jesus.'"*

Charles Stuart Beaty died on October 2, 2001, but his life continues to remind us that we must make the most of every opportunity to share Jesus Christ with a lost world.

* Quotes from Charles Beaty are used by permission of the International Mission Board. For more information visit www.tconline.org.

DAY 1
ALL ARE CALLED

You may still be asking, "But just who are the called? Are they a special group of persons? What about my life? Am I called too? How would I know? What would it sound like?"

And sincerely your heart may be saying, "Lord, I do love You! I do belong to You! I am Your servant, and I truly want to serve You. But Lord, am I really called to be on mission with You in my world? Lord, just who are the called?"

Unfortunately our "Christian culture" has not always been thoroughly biblical. That is, as we have made a difference between clergy and laypeople, so we have made a difference between the specially called and the common believer. **All are the called!** The differences lie not in whether we are called or not, but in the nature of the assignment given by God. But every believer is one who is called by God, for Him to be free to accomplish His purposes in them and through them!

Let's look briefly at some Scripture passages that assure us that every believer is called. In Exodus 19, when God created a special nation through whom He would bring salvation to the whole world, He said,

> *You have seen what I did to the Egyptians, and how I bore you on eagles' wings and brought you to Myself. Now therefore, if you will indeed obey My voice and keep My covenant, then you shall be a special*

UNFORTUNATELY, AS WE HAVE MADE A DIFFERENCE BETWEEN CLERGY AND LAYPEOPLE, SO WE HAVE MADE A DIFFERENCE BETWEEN THE SPECIALLY CALLED AND THE COMMON BELIEVER. ALL ARE THE CALLED!

> *treasure to Me above all people; for all the earth is Mine. And you shall be to Me a kingdom of priests and a holy nation. These are the words which you shall speak to the children of Israel.*
>
> EXODUS 19:4–6 (NKJV)

Read the Bible passages from Exodus, 1 Peter, and Acts found in the gray boxes. Express what it means for you to be part of a "kingdom of priests."

_____

_____

_____

_____

_____

_____

_____

_____

_____

_____

_____

He said they would be a kingdom of priests—not a kingdom with a priesthood. Each and every one of them would be priests unto God. The Levites would be the ones assigned to train and equip the entire nation to walk with God as priests unto God so He could fulfill His purposes to save the nations of the world through them. This same truth is stated in the New Testament.

> *You yourselves, as living stones, are being built into a spiritual house for a holy priesthood to offer spiritual sacrifices acceptable to God through Jesus Christ. . . . But you are a chosen race, a royal priesthood, a holy nation, a people for His possession, so that you may proclaim the praises of the One who called you out of darkness into His marvelous light. Once you were not a people, but now you are God's people; you had not received mercy, but now you have received mercy.*
>
> 1 PETER 2:5, 9–10 (HCSB)

Each believer is called of God and is to function before God and a watching world as a priest unto God. God, therefore, promised that He would enable every believer to function this way by the empowering presence of His Holy Spirit. At Pentecost God fulfilled that promise, and Peter announced to a deeply affected world:

> *This is what was spoken through the prophet Joel: "And it will be in the last days, says God, that I will pour out My Spirit on all humanity; then your sons and your daughters will prophesy, your young men will see visions, and your old men will dream dreams. I will even pour out My Spirit on My male and female slaves in those days; and they will prophesy."*
>
> ACTS 2:16–18 (HCSB)

From this Scripture it is obvious that God eternally planned that every believer would be spiritually equipped to both know and do the will of God, as He would reveal it to each one. God intended that none would function by themselves, but with the rest of God's people. The book of Acts records how God implemented His purposes through His people. It is very exciting to realize that this is what God is intending for each of us today. Each is saved, enabled by God's presence, and then incorporated into the people of God where God uniquely does His work through them.

THOUGHT FOR THE DAY

NEVER LOSE THE WONDER AND AWE OF GOD'S PURPOSES BEING WORKED OUT, FIRST IN YOU, AND THEN THROUGH YOU, FOR HIS GLORY.

How would you describe God's call?

_____

_____

_____

_____

_____

_____

_____

DAY 2
COMPLETENESS OF HIS CALL

Notice the extensiveness and completeness of God's call and God's equipping of all people—sons, daughters, young men and women, and old men and women. This includes your life also.

It is also interesting and encouraging to realize that throughout the Bible most of the people God calls and works through mightily are what we today would call *every believer*. They were very ordinary people called and enabled by God to work with Him in their world. Their abilities or skills were not as important as their relationship with God. Their heart relationship of love and trust in God always determined how much God was able to do through them.

David was a shepherd (see Psalm 78:70–72), and God chose him for a special assignment, in which God would guide His people through him.

According to Scripture, Amos said he was:

> **No prophet, nor was I a son of a prophet, but I was a sheepbreeder and a tender of sycamore fruit. Then the Lord took me as I followed the flock, and the Lord said to me, "Go, prophesy to My people Israel."**
> AMOS 7:14–15 (NKJV)

Peter was a fisherman, and all the others were what we would call "just ordinary people"—until God assigned them roles in His kingdom where He would work through them mightily to

THEIR ABILITIES OR SKILLS WERE NOT AS IMPORTANT AS THEIR RELATIONSHIP WITH GOD.

He also chose David His servant, and took him from the sheepfolds; From following the ewes that had young He brought him, to shepherd Jacob His people, and Israel His inheritance. So he shepherded them according to the integrity of his heart, and guided them by the skillfulness of his hands.
PSALM 78:70–72

accomplish His purposes. This has continued to be God's way to this very day. I watched God do this for more than thirty years as I served as a pastor (shepherd) among God's ordinary people.

How ordinary is your life compared to God's special assignment for you?

_____

_____

_____

_____

_____

_____

_____

_____

_____

_____

I remember Arthur and Marion. They were in their seventies when they came to me as their pastor. They felt God wanted to use them in starting a mission church in a Russian community. Arthur had been an accountant all of his life. He had been a deacon, and Marion had always served faithfully by his side. Now God was asking them in retirement to be available to Him for His larger purposes.

Arthur took 16 courses from the seminary extension department and received his pastoral ministries certificate in preparation for serving as our mission pastor. They served for six years, winning many scores of people to the Lord in one of the most difficult communities around us. We ordained Arthur at age 76. That year he also taught younger men in our theological college in the areas of accounting and finances. That same year he died of cancer, believing that the best years of his life were the last years as God worked through him and his wife to win a lost world to Himself. They were just ordinary Christians, available for God to work through them.

Alex worked in a steel plant, but God asked him to do church planting also. Alex and Eileen made their lives available to God and were used wonderfully to begin a new mission church in a needy community.

Melvin worked for Sears for 26 years. His wife was a practical nurse. In their fifties they sensed that God wanted them to use the next years of their lives in missions. They volunteered to be dorm parents for missionaries' kids (MKs) in Zambia. They were accepted, and spent the next eight years building the residence and caring for the children. Melvin also directed a successful Bible correspondence course that enrolled over 100,000 persons, with thousands of people coming to know Christ as their Savior.

All these examples are of ordinary people who knew that God has a right to use their lives in His time and place. They simply responded to God.

THOUGHT FOR THE DAY

GOD HAS NO LOOSE ENDS IN HIS ETERNAL PLAN! WHEN HE TOUCHES YOUR LIFE, IT IS A PART OF A COMPLETE AND THOROUGH STRATEGY, AND THE RESPONSE OF EACH PERSON (INCLUDING YOURS) IS VITAL TO THE *BIGGER PICTURE*.

Is God giving you a change of direction? If so, make a few notes that give evidence of God's direction. If you have not received a change of direction, how is God affirming what He has already called you to do?

_____

_____

_____

_____

_____

_____

_____

_____

_____

_____

DAY 3
JESUS EQUIPS THE CALLED

You may be thinking that you are not equipped to do this. Remember, in John 17 Jesus revealed to us that the Father gives our lives to Jesus for Him to develop and teach us. For what purpose? To make us useful vessels that His Father can use to save a lost and dying world. In that significant prayer, Jesus said to the Father:

> *I have glorified You on the earth by completing the work You gave Me to do. . . . I have revealed Your name to the men You gave Me from the world. They were Yours, You gave them to Me, and they have kept Your word. Now they know that all things You have given to Me are from You, because the words that You gave to Me, I have given to them. They have received them and have known for certain that I came from You. They have believed that You sent Me. . . . I have given them the glory that You have given to me. May they be one just as We are one. I am in them and You are in Me. May they be made completely one, so that the world may know You sent Me and that You have loved them just as You have loved Me.*
>
> JOHN 17:4, 6–8, 22–23 (HCSB)

When Jesus called the first disciples, He assured them of His responsibility for their lives by saying to them, "*Follow Me . . . and I will make you into fishers of men*" (Mark 1:17). Again He said to them, "*This is the will of Him who sent Me: that I should lose none of those He has given Me but should raise them up on the last day*" (John 6:39). All of the Gospels record how Jesus taught, trained, guided, encouraged, empowered, and fully equipped His disciples for all God had in mind to do through them.

How has Jesus:
taught you

_____

_____

trained you

_____

_____

guided you

_____

_____

encouraged you

_____

_____

empowered you

_____

_____

equipped you

_____

_____

John 17 reveals just how thoroughly Jesus prepared them for their mission in their world. Your life and mine are included in that very prayer in John 17.

As Jesus said, "*I pray not only for these, but also for those who believe in Me through their message*" (John 17:20). So you need not be concerned that you are not prepared to be of use to God. Our living Lord has accepted your life from the Father and is at work "making you to become" all God wants you to be.

OUR LIVING LORD HAS ACCEPTED YOUR LIFE FROM THE FATHER AND IS AT WORK "MAKING YOU TO BECOME" ALL GOD WANTS YOU TO BE.

THOUGHT FOR THE DAY

NO BELIEVER SHOULD LET FEAR OF FAILURE PREVENT THEM FROM RESPONDING FULLY TO THE CALL OF GOD. EVERYTHING NEEDED FOR LIFE AND GODLINESS HAS BEEN PROVIDED AND IS IMMEDIATELY AT WORK IN EVERY LIFE THAT OBEYS GOD'S CALL:

"*MAY GRACE AND PEACE BE MULTIPLIED TO YOU THROUGH THE KNOWLEDGE OF GOD AND OF JESUS OUR LORD. FOR HIS DIVINE POWER HAS GIVEN US EVERYTHING REQUIRED FOR LIFE AND GODLINESS, THROUGH THE KNOWLEDGE OF HIM WHO CALLED US BY HIS OWN GLORY AND GOODNESS. BY THESE HE HAS GIVEN US VERY GREAT AND PRECIOUS PROMISES, SO THAT THROUGH THEM YOU MAY SHARE IN THE DIVINE NATURE, ESCAPING THE CORRUPTION THAT IS IN THE WORLD BECAUSE OF EVIL DESIRES.*"
—*2 PETER 1:2–4*

How has Christ equipped and trained you?

_____

_____

_____

_____

_____

DAY 4
YOU ARE IMPORTANT TO GOD!

Each one of us is important to God! We are ordinary people who love God with all our hearts, and who know that the call to salvation is also a call to be laborers together with God in our world. As we respond to the call of God in a yielding to Him, He powerfully accomplishes His purpose to save a lost world through our lives. God seeks out those who are willing to "stand before Him on behalf of the land."

> *"So I sought for a man among them who would make a wall, and stand in the gap before Me on behalf of the land, that I should not destroy it; but I found no one. Therefore I have poured out My indignation on them; I have consumed them with the fire of my wrath; and I have recompensed their deeds on their own heads," says the Lord God.*
> EZEKIEL 22:30–31 (NKJV)

If He cannot find a person to "*stand in the gap*," the land and the people are destroyed. But when He does find someone who will go for us, He is able to save multitudes of people.

When Jonah finally obeyed God's assignment to take His message to the people of the great city of Nineveh, the king and all the people responded with immediate and thorough repentance, and the entire city was saved. This was the heart of God, and it waited on the obedience of an ordinary child of God. We must always ask ourselves, "What could have

GOD SEEKS OUT THOSE WHO ARE WILLING TO "STAND BEFORE HIM ON BEHALF OF THE LAND."

been if only I had responded immediately to God's invitation to join Him, and His heart, for the lost?"

Esther was a very ordinary woman. But she had "*come to the kingdom for such a time as this*" (Esther 4:13–14). Her response was vital—to the heart of God for His people. Their lives and destiny hung in the balance, and in the hand of Esther. She literally risked her life—but God worked through her to save His people. And we know of her life and deed to this very day. Many women were just as vital.

Hannah would bring forth the great prophet and judge, Samuel. Deborah saved God's people from their enemy (Judges 4, 5). Elizabeth and Mary were available to God for the bringing of John the Baptist and Jesus. And Mary Magdalene was greatly used of God, one day at a time, to minister to Jesus and His disciples, and was therefore greatly honored of God.

Can you call to the Lord and say to Him what Isaiah said?

> ***Also I heard the voice of the Lord, saying: "Whom shall I send, and who will go for Us?" Then I said, "Here am I! Send me."***
> ISAIAH 6:8 (NKJV)

And realize that,

> ***The eyes of the Lord run to and fro throughout the whole earth, to show Himself strong on behalf of those whose heart is loyal to Him.***
> 2 CHRONICLES 16:9 (NKJV)

And Mordecai told them to answer Esther: "Do not think in your heart that you will escape in the king's palace any more than all the other Jews. For if you remain completely silent at this time, relief and deliverance will arise for the Jews from another place, but you and your father's house will perish. Yet who knows whether you have come to the kingdom for such a time as this?"
ESTHER 4:13–14

So deep is the love of God for our lost world that the Spirit of God "*works in you both to will and to do for His good pleasure*" (Philippians 2:13, NKJV).

What has God put on your heart that requires an immediate response?

_____

_____

_____

_____

_____

_____

_____

_____

_____

_____

Gerry and Brenda Wortman had not been married long. Gerry had just become a Christian. As they studied their Bible, seeking to be faithful, they realized that they must be as prepared and as available to God as possible. This is what the Scriptures revealed to them. They came to attend the theological college we had established in our church to gain some basic knowledge of God and His Word. As they studied, God saw their hearts, and through unusual circumstances led them to respond to a First Nations reservation in Canada to teach the Bible. By the time they completed their three years of study, God had given them a heart for the native peoples and the special skill to enable them to minister to them.

God reached many people through Gerry and Brenda. Later they were called to pastor a mission for First Nations people, and then to a position directing First Nations ministries for all Canada. Currently, Gerry is a pastor of a church in Saskatchewan, and of course the church has several ministries to First Nations peoples. He and Brenda have also adopted four First Nations children!

Two lives were called to salvation, and they realized that the call to salvation was a call to be fully available for God's purpose to win a lost world, wherever He would choose to send them. What a difference they have made! And that sense of purpose has captured their lives.

THOUGHT FOR THE DAY

YOU CAN NEVER FULLY ESTIMATE THE VALUE OF YOUR LIFE TO GOD. TO GOD, ETERNITY IS ALWAYS AT STAKE! YOUR OBEDIENCE RELEASES THE FULLNESS OF GOD IN ACCOMPLISHING HIS PURPOSE TO REDEEM A LOST WORLD AND EVEN TO INAUGURATE ETERNITY IN HIS FULLNESS OF TIME.

Do you sense that the Spirit of God is working in your life, causing you to want to do His will and promising to help you accomplish His will? How would you describe it?

DAY 5
TAKING A SPIRITUAL INVENTORY

Now is an appropriate time to do what I call "taking a spiritual inventory"! The inventory is found on pages 71-72, and you'll be asked to complete it at the end of today's study. The inventory will help you evaluate, in light of all the Scriptures you have honestly pursued with the Holy Spirit as your teacher, how you are doing.

Such an inventory is necessary for the sincere believer! Too often Christians want to have, for example, the "faith of Abraham." But they do not realize that it took God about forty years to develop Abraham's character to the point where he would immediately respond to God's command to offer his only son, Isaac, as a "sacrifice to God." During those years of development, God often reviewed His covenant with Abraham, found in Genesis 12:1–4. He also brought Moses constantly before Him to remind him of Moses' walk with God. He did this with David as well, and in Psalm 51 we see the major changes David had to make to "restore to [him] the joy of His salvation" (v.12). And Jesus had to take His disciples aside constantly to explain how their continuing lack of faith was affecting their relationship with Him.

God must take each of us aside regularly, remind us of His call in our life, bring to our remembrance all He has said to us (John 14:26), and help us see how we are responding to His shaping and guiding of our lives.

A spiritual inventory must be done in the presence of God! He alone has Lordship in our lives. To Him alone are we accountable. Therefore, it is before Him and in His presence that we must stand for a spiritual evaluation—done by God. You may sense that He is saying, "Well done, good and faithful servant. You have been faithful in a little, I can now give you more!" Or, you may sense God is grieved, and is exclaiming, "Why do you keep calling Me 'Lord! Lord!' yet never do anything that I say?"

Paul assured believers that they could stand face to face with God, with "no veil" in between them and God. But he said that when they stood face to face with God they would be *transformed into the same image from glory to glory*" (2 Corinthians 3:18). When a believer is face to face with God there is an automatic "inventory" taken by God— Christlikeness! This standing before God comes when we, with transparent honesty, bring ourselves before the "*washing of water by the Word*" (Ephesians 5:26–27). The regular reading and study of God's Word is a *must* for every believer.

Now the LORD had said to Abram: "Get out of your country, from your family and from your father's house, to a land that I will show you. I will make you a great nation; I will bless you and make your name great; and you shall be a blessing. I will bless those who bless you, and I will curse him who curses you; and in you all the families of the earth shall be blessed." So Abram departed as the LORD had spoken to him, and Lot went with him. And Abram was seventy-five years old when he departed from Haran.
GENESIS 12:1–4

A SPIRITUAL INVENTORY MUST BE DONE IN THE PRESENCE OF GOD! HE ALONE HAS LORDSHIP IN OUR LIVES. TO HIM ALONE ARE WE ACCOUNTABLE.

Prayer also brings us into God's presence, where God changes our ways into His ways and we cry out as Jesus did, "*Not My will, but Thine be done!*"

In summary: here are the important ingredients of a "spiritual inventory":

1. Do it before God.

2. Do it with His Word and prayer as your "plumbline."

3. Do it with transparent honesty.

4. Do it thoroughly.

5. Ask the right questions:

   • Am I a believer?

   • Do I therefore know that I am called by God?

   • Does this include being on mission with God?

   • Does my life give constant evidence of this relationship with God?

THOUGHT FOR THE DAY

A SPIRITUAL INVENTORY MUST BE DONE IN THE PRESENCE OF GOD. IT IS GOD ALONE TO WHOM WE ARE ACCOUNTABLE.

What do these inventory questions reveal to you?

_____

_____

_____

_____

My Spiritual Inventory
Date: _____

HOW ARE YOU DOING WITH YOUR UNDERSTANDING OF GOD, AND OF HIS PURPOSES AND HIS WAYS?

_____

_____

_____

_____

_____

_____

_____

_____

HOW HAVE YOU RESPONDED TO WHAT YOU NOW KNOW OF GOD?

_____

_____

_____

_____

_____

_____

_____

_____

WHAT STRATEGIC CHANGES HAVE YOU ALREADY MADE IN YOUR LIFE AND YOUR LIFESTYLE SO THAT GOD MAY WORK IN AND THROUGH YOU?

_____

_____

_____

WHAT ACTIVITY OF GOD HAVE YOU ALREADY NOTICED TAKING PLACE IN YOUR LIFE?

WHAT EVIDENCES OF CHRISTLIKENESS DO YOU NOTICE TAKING PLACE IN YOUR LIFE, AND HOW ARE YOU RESPONDING TO THESE CHANGES?

Called & Accountable
Tillie Burgin

"Hang Out and Hover"

The phone rang in the Missions Office at First Baptist Church of Arlington, Texas. On the line was a woman who needed help paying her electric bill. That call led to the start of a ministry that touches thousands of lives each year. Tillie Burgin answered the call that day, and now she is director of Mission Arlington/Mission Metroplex.

Tillie helped the woman who called that day and also asked the woman to start a Bible study in her apartment. Seventeen people came to the first meeting! Soon Bible studies were starting in other apartment complexes. Tillie began to take "church" to people. Fifteen years later, Tillie, along with over 2,000 volunteers, is still taking church to people.

Over 3,700 attend 250 Bible studies each week. Another 28,000 receive food, clothing, furniture, and other assistance each month. Mission Arlington/Mission Metroplex also provides dental and medical care, crisis counseling, financial help, English classes, and day care. In 2001, 2,150 people received Christ as their Savior through this ministry.

Mission Arlington/Metroplex functions on a simple concept Tillie calls "hang out and hover." Volunteers find people, hang out with them to get to know them and their needs, and then hover around John 3:16. Because the gospel is for "whosoever," everyone is important and needs to hear the gospel.

Tillie grew up right across the street from First Baptist Church. From an early age, she wanted to be a missionary. In 1966 Tillie and her husband, Bob, along with their two sons, went to serve in South Korea as missionaries. Ten years later they resigned due to the health problems of their younger son and moved back to Arlington.

Tillie's heart was still in missions. She felt that if she could do missions in Korea, she could do missions in Arlington! And she is still "hanging out and hovering."

CALLED & ACCOUNTABLE

UNIT 4
HOW AM I CALLED?

Unit 4
How Am I Called?

Essential Truth for the Week

God rarely does the same thing twice, for He desires that every person believe *Him*, have faith in *Him*—not a *method*! Throughout the Bible and in history, through the testimony of those God has used mightily, every person's call has been deliberately *unique* to each believer.

CALLED & ACCOUNTABLE
HAROLD RAY WATSON

"A NEW WAY TO BE SALT"

In 1965 Harold Watson, his wife Joyce, and their three small boys arrived in M'lang, Cotabato, a small town in the center of Mindanao, the Philippines. Harold and his family had been appointed by the International Mission Board to be "agriculture evangelists" on the second-largest island in the Philippines.

Harold had never heard of agricultural evangelism while growing up on a farm in rural Mississippi. He did like farming and wondered if someday he might be able to have his own farm. While serving in the Air Force on the island of Okinawa during the Korean War, Harold believed that God was calling him to be a missionary. Harold began to think that there might be a new way to share the gospel of Jesus Christ in foreign lands through his love of farming.

Upon arriving in the Philippines, Harold observed that many of the Filipinos were impoverished and malnourished. Most of the steep land was not suited for traditional farming, so the people had little to eat and no way to make even a meager income. Harold decided to set up a demonstration farm on 50 acres of land and develop a method of farming that would help the Filipinos be able to help themselves.

The fifty acres of land became known as the Mindanao Baptist Rural Life Center. Harold gradually developed a farming method called SALT, Sloping Agricultural Land Technology, which enables local farmers to produce food on badly eroded hillsides. Training programs at the center introduce people to the new farming method and to Jesus Christ. The students return to their villages with the ability to provide physical and spiritual food for their families.

SALT has been adopted by a variety of countries and relief organizations to battle hunger, including Indonesia, Sri Lanka, Burma, and many other Asian countries. Some 18,000 people visit the center every year to learn SALT.

Jesus commanded His followers to be the "salt of the earth." God showed Harold Watson a new way to be salt in a lost world.

Day 1
Awareness of God's Call

For a Christian to ask seriously the question, "How am I called?" the Christian must bring with this question a personal commitment both to respond and to be accountable to God in the calling. When Christians sense that God is guiding them to a clear, simple answer to this question, they will also be deeply, even painfully aware that having the knowledge of His will brings with it immediately a solemn sense of accountability.

When you sense God is calling you, you can never be the same again! You will have to say, "Yes Lord!" Be aware that you may tend to say no. But you cannot say, "No Lord!" For if you say no at that moment, He is no longer Lord. For lordship means, by definition, always a yes. When Jesus is Lord, His servant always says, "Yes Lord!"

We have already indicated that the initial call is a call to salvation, a call to become a child of God and servant of Jesus Christ. It is an eternal decision and an eternal relationship. But from the moment when I am born again, how am I called by God in my mission with Him?

Many forget that when a person first becomes a Christian, they are a "baby" Christian, and they must then grow and learn to use their newly given "spiritual senses." They need to learn to function with their newly provided spiritual family, the local church. This takes time and experience, just as it does in the physical birth and growth experience.

The context for this growth, as designed and provided by

HAVING THE KNOWLEDGE OF HIS WILL BRINGS WITH IT IMMEDIATELY A SOLEMN SENSE OF ACCOUNTABILITY.

Not that I have already reached the goal, or am already fully mature; but I make every effort to take hold of it because I also have been taken hold of by Christ Jesus. Brothers, I do not consider myself to have taken hold of it. But one thing I do: forgetting what is behind and reaching forward to what is ahead, I pursue as my goal the prize promised by God's heavenly call in Christ Jesus. Therefore, all who are mature should think this way.

Philippians 3:12–15a

God, is the local church. God does not bring a person into His Kingdom without adequate provision for protection, learning, feeding, and being loved. In the local church we learn about our new life in Christ and are given the opportunities to learn to walk, talk, share, and gain experiences.

New believers must first receive the "*milk of the Word*" (1 Peter 2:2, NKJV). They are carefully taken from milk to meat (Hebrews 5:12–14). They should become teachers of the Word, and by skillful use of the Word move from milk to meat. The church must help each believer grow this way, becoming mature and able to be of greater and greater use to God. Paul constantly speaks of becoming "mature" (Philippians 3:12–16).

But all this takes time! It also takes complete obedience to Christ, who commanded believers not only to "make disciples" and "baptize them," but also to "teach them to observe everything I have commanded you" (Matthew 28:19–20). This task is most spiritually demanding but was faithfully practiced by early believers in Jerusalem, as seen in Acts 2:41–47. This is a simple and clear picture of a spiritual family, the local church, taking care of newborn believers. As you read the rest of the Book of Acts, you see how those believers soon were on mission with God all over their world. God really did accomplish His eternal purpose to redeem the lost through them.

Write the name of a person in your local church whom you are helping to mature. Begin praying for that person daily, asking God to help you know how to guide them.

A brief summary of the things that new believers must learn early in their Christian life would include:

- to receive spiritual food
- to develop their newly-given "spiritual senses" (more about this in Day 2's study)
- to develop a great sensitivity toward sin
- to learn the strategies of Satan (as Jesus did)
- to learn to resist Satan and sin with their whole being
- to know (often the hard way) the consequences of sin, and the crucial place of the church in restoring them
- to know the nature of a life of holiness, so they will always be available to God
- to know their place in the Body (local church) and how their lives are used by God to edify and grow others in the Body
- to find out, as the disciples did, the nature of the Kingdom of Heaven, and how God functions in their world, especially by prayer

Having grown up in Christ, they will be gradually taken on mission with God. As they are faithful in little things, God will give them more and more significant opportunities to be on mission with Him. In this process they will learn to "wait on the Lord"—to "be still." In this waiting they will come to learn to:

1. Yield their lives completely to God's working through them.

2. Appropriate all that God has provided by His grace and by His presence with them. This will include especially Christ living out His life in them, and the complete sufficiency of the presence and power of the Holy Spirit.

All this, and much more, is involved in an awareness of God's call.

THOUGHT FOR THE DAY

TO BE AWARE OF GOD'S CALL WHEN ONE BECOMES A CHRISTIAN IS LIFE'S GREATEST GIFT FROM GOD. TO FULFILL THIS CALL WILL BE LIFE'S GREATEST ACHIEVEMENT.

What is your history of saying, "Yes, Lord?"

_____

_____

_____

_____

_____

_____

_____

_____

DAY 2
SPIRITUAL SENSES DEVELOPED

First, remember that when you are born again as a child of God, you are given spiritual senses (Matthew 13:10–23) so you can hear and see and understand all the ways and activities of God.

Then the disciples came up and asked Him, "Why do you speak to them in parables?"

He answered them, "To know the secrets of the kingdom of heaven has been granted to you, but to them it has not been granted. For whoever has, more will be given to him, and he will have more than enough. But whoever does not have, even what he has will be taken away from him. For this reason I speak to them in parables, because looking they do not see, and hearing they do not listen or understand.

"In them the prophecy of Isaiah is fulfilled that says:

'You will listen and listen, yet never understand; and you will look and look, yet never perceive. For this people's heart has grown callous; their ears are hard of hearing, and they have shut their eyes; otherwise they might see with their eyes and hear with their ears, understand with their hearts and turn back—and I would cure them.'

"But your eyes are blessed because they do see, and your ears because they do hear! For I assure you: Many prophets and righteous people longed to

see the things you see, yet didn't see them; to hear the things you hear, yet didn't hear them.

"You, then, listen to the parable of the sower:

"When anyone hears the word about the kingdom and doesn't understand it, the evil one comes and snatches away what was sown in his heart. This is the one sown along the path.

"And the one sown on rocky ground—this is one who hears the word and immediately receives it with joy. Yet he has no root in himself, but is short-lived. When pressure or persecution comes because of the word, immediately he stumbles.

"Now the one sown among the thorns—this is one who hears the word, but the worries of this age and the pleasure of wealth choke the word, and it becomes unfruitful.

"But the one sown on the good ground—this is one who hears and understands the word, who does bear fruit and yields: some a hundred, some sixty, some thirty times what was sown."

MATTHEW 13:10–23 (HCSB)

Jesus clearly indicated to His disciples that since they had been "called by God," they were different in several significant ways:

"To know the secrets of the kingdom of heaven has been granted to you, but to them [others around them] *it has not been granted"* (Matthew 13:11). This was followed by this astounding announcement: *"But your eyes are blessed*

because they do see, and your ears because they do hear" (Matthew 13:16). But every believer must develop the use of these special spiritual senses. It is by the use of them that one grows (Hebrews 5:13–14).

A newborn child is fully equipped with senses to function in the physical world. By the constant use of them, a child grows to maturity. I had to assist each of my children to use their eyes to see, their ears to hear, and their noses to smell. At each stage of their growth, they had new things to learn. I knew that if they grew normally, they could read and eventually attain to a Ph.D., if God called them to that task. My oldest son, Richard, did get his Ph.D., pastored a church, and was later called to be the president of our Canadian Baptist Theological Seminary, where he is doing a great job to this day. But the day-by-day growth when he was younger was essential to what he would become.

Every believer must be helped to develop their spiritual senses, given to them by God. It is crucial to their development and their later usefulness to God. The local church is a major factor, as are the believers God places around them at spiritual birth.

Each child of God must learn to hear and recognize the voice of God, and obey Him. Jesus assured the disciples that this would be true, when He said:

> **The one who enters by the door is the shepherd of the sheep. The doorkeeper opens it for him, and the sheep hear his voice. He calls his own sheep by name**

Now everyone who lives on milk is inexperienced with the message about righteousness, because he is an infant. But solid food is for the mature— for those whose senses have been trained to distinguish between good and evil.
HEBREWS 5:13–14

EACH CHILD OF GOD MUST LEARN TO HEAR AND RECOGNIZE THE VOICE OF GOD, AND OBEY HIM.

> *and leads them out. When he has brought all his own outside, he goes ahead of them. The sheep follow him because they recognize his voice. . . . My sheep hear My voice, I know them, and they follow Me.*
> JOHN 10:2–4, 27 (HCSB)

EVERY SHEEP WHO IS A PART OF HIS FLOCK KNOWS THE SHEPHERD'S VOICE AND FOLLOWS HIM. OTHER SHEEP IN THE SAME FOLD CAN ASSIST THE LAMBS AS THEY LEARN THIS SKILL.

Every sheep who is a part of His flock knows the Shepherd's voice and follows Him. Other sheep in the same fold can assist the lambs as they learn this skill.

How do you know when the Shepherd is speaking to you?

_____

_____

_____

_____

_____

_____

_____

_____

Each child of God must learn to "see" the activity of God and join Him. This Jesus did, and each believer must also.

> *Jesus answered, "I assure you: Unless someone is born again, he cannot see the kingdom of God."*
> JOHN 3:3 (HCSB)

A servant sees where the Master is, and joins Him.

> *If anyone serves Me, he must follow Me. Where I am, there My servant also will be. If anyone serves Me, the Father will honor him.*
>
> JOHN 12:26 (HCSB)

The servant does not take the initiative; the Master does. The servant has died to self and come alive to his Lord.

> *I assure you: Unless a grain of wheat falls into the ground and dies, it remains by itself. But if it dies, it produces a large crop. The one who loves his life will lose it, and the one who hates his life in this world will keep it for eternal life.*
>
> JOHN 12:24–25 (HCSB)

And every believer must learn to understand with their heart and obey Him.

> *But the Counselor, the Holy Spirit, whom the Father will send in My name, will teach you all things and remind you of everything I have told you.*
>
> JOHN 14:26 (HCSB)

God is always looking at the heart, for out of the heart the entire life proceeds. This is why Jesus asked Peter this life-determining question: "Peter, do you love Me?"

> *"Simon, son of John, do you love Me more than these?"*
>
> *"Yes, Lord," he said to Him, "You know that I love you."*
>
> *"Feed My lambs," He told him.*
>
> *A second time He asked him, "Simon, son of John, do you love Me?"*
>
> *"Yes, Lord," he said to Him, "You know that I love you."*
>
> *"Shepherd My sheep," He told him.*
>
> *He asked him the third time, "Simon, son of John, do you love Me?"*
>
> *Peter was grieved that He asked him the third time, "Do you love Me?" He said, "Lord, You know everything! You know that I love You."*
>
> *"Feed My sheep," Jesus said.*
>
> JOHN 21:15–17 (HCSB)

But you must develop your spiritual senses by use (Hebrews 5:13–14). As a child is fully equipped with physical senses to function in the physical world, so the Christian is given spiritual senses to function in the spiritual world in our relationship with God.

Look up the following verses and write how our spiritual senses help our relationship with God.

1. **We can learn to hear His voice and follow Him.**

    (John 10:2–4, 27)

2. We can learn to see His activity and join Him.

(John 3:3; 5:17:19–20)

_____

_____

3. We can learn to understand with our hearts and obey Him.

(John 14:26; 16:13–15)

_____

_____

Just as a little child learns to function in our world a little at a time, if we are faithful in a little, He will give us more (Luke 16:10). Jesus said that when we hear and then obey, we are like a man building his house on a rock—nothing can shake it or destroy it (Luke 6:46–49).

There are some things that must be firmly in place in the Christian's life to experience the fullness of God's calling in life.

THOUGHT FOR THE DAY

IF A CHRISTIAN DOES NOT KNOW WHEN GOD IS SPEAKING TO HIM, HE IS IN TROUBLE AT THE HEART OF HIS RELATIONSHIP WITH GOD. IF THIS IS A DIFFICULTY TO YOU, STOP EVERYTHING ELSE, AND ASK GOD TO TEACH YOU UNTIL YOU ARE CERTAIN OF HIS VOICE.

"Why do you call Me 'Lord, Lord,' and don't do the things I say? I will show you what someone is like who comes to Me, hears My words, and acts on them: He is like a man building a house, who dug deep and laid the foundation on the rock. When the flood rose, the river crashed against that house and couldn't shake it, because it was well built. But the one who hears and does not act is like a man who built a house on the ground without a foundation. The river crashed against it, and immediately it collapsed. And the destruction of that house was great!"
LUKE 6:46–49

What do you believe must be in place in your life if you are to experience the fullness of God's calling?

_____

_____

_____

_____

_____

_____

_____

_____

DAY 3
YOU MUST CLEARLY KNOW HIM

A person must clearly and unmistakably know God. Jesus said eternal life was coming to "*know You, the only true God, and the One You have sent—Jesus Christ*" (John 17:3). This means you clearly have come to receive Jesus Christ into your life as your personal Savior and Lord.

So crucial was this thorough knowledge of Jesus Christ to the purposes of God that the Father taught the disciples through Jesus how to have this relationship. It was almost three years into Jesus' ministry before Jesus finally asked them, "*who do you say that I am?*" (Matthew 16:15). When Peter responded that He was the Christ, the Son of the Living

God, Jesus assured him that *"flesh and blood did not reveal this to you, but My Father in heaven"* (Matthew 16:17). Only then, with the disciples fully committed to who He was, was He able for the first time to introduce them to His cross, and His coming death (Matthew 16:21).

Describe who Jesus is to you.

_____

_____

_____

_____

_____

_____

_____

_____

Without this God-given heart understanding of who Jesus is, all else is useless. It is such a part of the Father's plan. But it is not merely "head knowledge." It must be the heart! The heart determines every other response to God. On our response rests the eternal purpose of God, being worked out through us.

THOUGHT FOR THE DAY

EVERY BELIEVER MUST HAVE A THOROUGH, GOD-GIVEN, REAL, AND PERSONAL RELATIONSHIP WITH JESUS CHRIST. THE ENTIRE CHRISTIAN LIFE DEPENDS ON IT!

Write out the testimony of when you surrendered your life to Christ.

_____

_____

_____

_____

_____

_____

_____

_____

_____

_____

_____

_____

_____

_____

_____

_____

_____

_____

_____

_____

_____

_____

_____

Day 4
Accountability to God

Just as simply as a little child, you must daily believe Him. That is, "*the one who draws near to Him must believe that He exists and He rewards those who seek Him*" (Hebrews 11:6*b*). This is because "*without faith it is impossible to please God*" (Hebrews 11:6*a*). Therefore, the believer must accept as true all God has revealed about Himself, especially in Scripture, and accept as binding upon his life all He has said, asked, or commanded. Since God is indeed God, His child believes Him and obeys Him.

With all his heart, mind, soul, and strength, a child of God loves Him, and therefore trusts Him, and responds unconditionally to Him. Paul did this in his life, and discovered and bore witness that the love of Christ compelled [constrained] him (2 Corinthians 5:14).

In this same chapter in 2 Corinthians, Paul expressed his sense of accountability to God:

> *Therefore, whether we are at home or away, we make it our aim to be pleasing to Him. For we must all appear before the judgment seat of Christ, so that each may be repaid for what he has done in the body, whether good or bad. Knowing then, the fear of the Lord, we persuade people. We are completely open before God, and I hope we are completely open to your consciences as well.*
>
> 2 Corinthians 5:9–11 (HCSB)

He also added that when he was saved, God not only reconciled him to Himself, but committed to him and all believers *"the message of reconciliation . . . . Therefore, we are ambassadors for Christ; certain that God is appealing through us, we plead on Christ's behalf, "Be reconciled to God"* (2 Corinthians 5:19–20).

Jesus had clearly indicated to His disciples (see Matthew 25) that there would be a time of accountability with God. It is a serious time before God. And He will reward everyone according to his faithful obedience to the Master. Each will hear his Lord and Master say, *"Well done, good and faithful slave! You were faithful over a few things; I will put you in charge of many things. Enter your Master's joy"* (Matthew 25:23).

Is there an area of your life in which Jesus would not say "Well done"? What is it?

_____

_____

_____

_____

_____

_____

_____

_____

_____

But it is certainly clear that our accountability is not just at the Judgment, but in this life also. As we are faithful in a little, He gives us more. What an anticipation as a faithful servant of Jesus Christ!

THOUGHT FOR THE DAY

TO LIVE WITHOUT A REAL SENSE OF ACCOUNTABILITY IS TO LOSE A MAJOR MOTIVATION IN SERVING OUR LORD! JUST TO KNOW THAT NOT A THING WE DO GOES WITHOUT HIS NOTICE AND LOVE BRINGS COMFORT. TO LOVE HIM WITH ALL OUR HEART, SOUL, MIND, AND STRENGTH BRINGS WITH IT SUCH AN INTIMATE RELATIONSHIP AND SPONTANEOUS, JOYFUL ACCOUNTABILITY. ALL THOSE WHO HAVE BEEN GREATLY USED OF GOD LIVED THIS WAY.

What sense of God's accountability are you living with?

Day 5
You Must Obey Him

Unhesitatingly and immediately you will obey Him. Jesus said, "*If anyone loves Me, he will obey My teaching. My Father will love him, and We will come to him and make Our home with him. He who does not love Me will not obey My teaching*" (John 14:23–24, NIV).

The Holy Spirit, your enabler, will assist you in hearing and knowing the call and will of God. He will do this all through your life (read John 14:25–26; John 16:13–15; Romans 8:26; 1 Corinthians 2:10–16).

Read the passages listed above. How has God assisted you in knowing the call and will of God?

_____

_____

_____

_____

_____

_____

_____

_____

Our oldest son Richard first came to know the Lord as a young boy. We were confident that if we would instruct him to listen to the Lord, and if we would create the spiritual atmosphere in which God could speak to him, that Richard would respond.

While a teenager, he came forward in a worship service saying, "Dad, I've known that God was calling me, but I have been running from the Lord. I come now to say 'yes' to God's call for me to be His servant. I think I might be a pastor."

He then began answering God's continuing call by serving as president of the youth group, as Baptist Student Ministry (BSM) president, and then BSM state president. After graduation he went to seminary, being called of God to Southwestern Baptist Theological Seminary. Then a further call came to enter the Ph.D. program and write a history of Canadian Southern Baptist work. Then he responded to God's call to pastor Friendship Baptist Church in Winnipeg, Manitoba, Canada.

He continues to experience daily the call of God in his life, aided, taught, and enabled to do it by the Spirit of God. As a matter of fact, all five of our children (four boys and one girl) have sensed the call of God to ministry or missions, and continue to openly respond to God's daily claim on their lives.

Within the family and the church family, the spiritual atmosphere is created where the ordinary Christian can hear the call of God and respond confidently. Here the call of God is clarified and the Christian is assisted to obey God's call.

The missions organizations of the church have a key role

WITHIN THE CHURCH FAMILY, THE CHRISTIAN CAN HEAR THE CALL OF GOD AND RESPOND CONFIDENTLY. HERE THE CALL OF GOD IS CLARIFIED AND THE CHRISTIAN IS ASSISTED TO OBEY GOD'S CALL.

in creating this spiritual atmosphere, so that every believer can experience his or her calling and carry it out in a responsible, effective way. The missions organizations provide opportunities for Bible study, missions study, missions activities, personal involvement, models for missions, and ministry and service opportunities. It is therefore in the midst of serving our Lord that His call is clarified. When His call is clarified, we can respond with obedience!

Linda and Renee came to our association as volunteer missionaries. They had sensed the call of God to come and spend two years with us. During these two years, we sought to create a spiritual atmosphere in which God could have the maximum opportunity to reveal to each of them the next step in His claim on and call for their lives. We spent time in Bible study and answering questions. They were given assignments that they sensed were from the Lord, and they responded eagerly. We walked with them through the disappointments, failures, victories, and the painful and happy times.

Their assignment ended in the fall of 1986. Renee went on to other missions assignments and is now completing seminary training in preparation for a life of ministry. Linda went on to direct the Southern Baptist witness to the Winter Olympics in Calgary, Alberta, then to serve in New York, and is now taking seminary courses in the Northeast in preparation for a life of being on mission with her Lord.

The "how" of being called of God came for both Renee and Linda in the midst of their personal relationship with God and His people as they followed their Lord daily.

THOUGHT FOR THE DAY

EVERYTHING IN THE CHRISTIAN'S LIFE RESTS ON OBEDIENCE! OBEDIENCE ALWAYS UNLOCKS THE ACTIVITY OF GOD IN A CHRISTIAN'S LIFE. OBEDIENCE IS WHERE ALL THE REAL ACTIVITY OF GOD ON MISSION REALLY BEGINS. OBEDIENCE IS THE ESSENTIAL HEART OF EXPERIENCING A LIFE ON MISSION WITH GOD IN THE WORLD.

In what area of your life is the Holy Spirit, your enabler, currently assisting you in hearing and knowing the call and will of God?

CALLED & ACCOUNTABLE
PANDITA RAMABAI

"NOTHING TO FEAR, NOTHING TO LOSE, NOTHING TO REGRET"

Women in India in the late 19th and early 20th centuries lived in hopelessness and despair. They were denied education, looked upon as slaves in their Hindu culture, and not allowed to acquire a trade or other means of livelihood.

Into this culture Pandita Ramabai was born in 1858 in Gangamul, India. At 23, Ramabai experienced the deplorable treatment of Indian women firsthand; her husband of 2 years died, leaving her with a daughter to raise and an uncertain future at the bottom of Indian society.

Ramabai's plight caused her to reexamine her Hindu faith. She began a quest to find the true God who could provide her a hope and a future. After many years of searching, Ramabai embraced Jesus Christ. She read biographies of George Mueller and Hudson Taylor and wondered if it were not possible to work in India as these men had in other countries. So Ramabai began to let her Lord guide her to help the women of India.

In 1889 she founded *Sharada Sadan*, a shelter for destitute women and orphans, and soon after another shelter named *Mukti*, meaning "salvation or deliverance." Through these institutions, Ramabai provided food, clothing, shelter, education, and job training for these women and orphans. More importantly, Ramabai introduced them to her living Lord.

Although Ramabai was responsible for the physical and spiritual care of thousands of women and orphans, she found that God was more than capable of handling the assignment He had given her.

She once said: "We are not rich, nor great, but we are happy, getting our daily bread directly from the loving hands of our heavenly Father, having not a piece over and above our daily necessities, having no banking account anywhere, no endowment or income from any earthly source, but depending altogether on our Father God, we have nothing to fear from anybody, nothing to lose, and nothing to regret."

Though Ramabai died in 1922, the works she established continue to this day, a testimony to the faithfulness of her Lord she loved and served.

CALLED & ACCOUNTABLE

UNIT 5
WHEN AM I CALLED?

UNIT 5
WHEN AM I CALLED?

ESSENTIAL TRUTH FOR THE WEEK

God is God! When He speaks, He also ensures that you will hear and will know His call. Your heart will be revealed in your response to Him.

John 6:43— *Jesus answered them, "Stop complaining among yourselves."*

John 6:44— *"No one can come to Me unless the Father who sent Me draws him, and I will raise him up on the last day."*

John 6:64— *"But there are some among you who don't believe." (For Jesus knew from the beginning those who would not believe and the one who would betray Him.)*

John 14:21— *"The one who has My commandments and keeps them is the one who loves Me. And the one who loves Me will be loved by My Father. I also will love him and will reveal Myself to him."*

John 14:23— *Jesus answered, "If anyone loves Me, he will keep My word. My Father will love him, and We will come to him and make Our home with him."*

John 14:24— *"The one who doesn't love Me will not keep My words. The word that you hear is not Mine, but is from the Father who sent Me."*

CALLED & ACCOUNTABLE
WILLIAM WILBERFORCE

CREATED FOR A PURPOSE

William Wilberforce was born in Hull, England, in 1759 into a family of wealth and status. He attended St. John's College in Cambridge but was not very interested in studying. Although Wilberforce was interested in politics, he had no real sense of purpose for his political desires.

Wilberforce entered politics and was elected to the House of Commons on his first try at the age of 21. He accomplished very little his first few years in office.

In his late twenties, however, Wilberforce began to reflect on the direction and purpose of his life. While on a tour of Europe he read William Law's book, *A Serious Call to a Devout and Holy Life*. This book led to Wilberforce's spiritual rebirth. As Wilberforce considered leaving politics and entering the ministry, he became persuaded that his true purpose and calling was to serve God through his political life.

Wilberforce became a very powerful advocate for social and moral reform in England. He worked tirelessly for the care of orphans, chimney sweeps, refugees, and prisoners. He was also very involved in mission and Bible societies. Wilberforce also shared his spiritual rebirth in a book entitled *A Practical View of the Prevailing Religious System of Professed Christians*, encouraging a return to God and a life of holiness and concern for the welfare of others.

Wilberforce became known primarily for his commitment to the abolition of the slave trade and slavery. Though he faced tremendous political opposition as well as terrible personal attacks, Wilberforce continued his anti-slavery efforts. He introduced his first anti-slavery motion in 1788 and continued to do so for eighteen years until the slave trade was finally abolished in 1806. He continued to fight for the abolition of slavery itself and was able to claim victory just a few days before his death in 1833.

The legacy of William Wilberforce lies not only in the causes he stood for and the victories he won, but also in what God can do through anyone who realizes and lives out God's purpose for his life.

DAY 1
KNOWING THE CALL

The Bible reveals, as we study carefully the lives of those God used significantly, that it is when we are in the midst of God's activity in our world that we most clearly know the call of God for our lives. A most significant verse to help us understand this is found in the life and witness of Jesus. He said:

> *But Jesus responded to them, "My Father is still working, and I also am working." . . . Then Jesus replied, "I assure you: The Son is not able to do anything on His own, but only what He sees the Father doing. For whatever the Father does, these things the Son also does in the same way. For the Father loves the Son and shows Him everything He is doing, and He will show Him greater works than these so that you will be amazed."*
>
> JOHN 5:17, 19–20 (HCSB)

First, Jesus said that it was the Father who was at work in the world. Jesus was His chosen servant. Jesus said the Son (servant) does not take the initiative, but rather watches to see where the Father (Master) is working and joins Him. But Jesus said the Father loves the Son, and therefore shows Him everything that He Himself is doing. The Son joins in with the Father, working together with Him. It is then that the Father is able to complete all He has purposed to do through the Son. This is how God purposed to bring a lost world back to Himself. He does it through His Son who loves, trusts, and obeys the Father. Listen to what the Scriptures say concerning the enormous price God and His Son paid for this great salvation.

> *During His earthly life, He offered prayers and appeals, with loud cries and tears, to the One who was able to save Him from death, and He was heard because of His reverence. Though a Son, He learned obedience through what He suffered. After He was perfected, He became the source of eternal salvation to all who obey Him.*
>
> HEBREWS 5:7–9 (HCSB)

Every person through whom God is able to work mightily has lived out this kind of relationship with God. Amos, the prophet, was a layman (a shepherd and a caretaker of sycamore-fig trees). He said,

> *I was no prophet, nor was I a son of a prophet, but I was a sheepbreeder and a tender of sycamore fruit. Then the LORD took me as I followed the flock, and the LORD said to me, "Go, prophesy to My people Israel."*
>
> AMOS 7:14–15 (NKJV)

God had an urgent message that His people, Israel, needed to hear immediately! Time was running out on them. Judgment was very near them. God wanted them to hear from Him and

His love one more time! Amos was the man God chose to take His message to His people. It surprised Amos, but he responded obediently, and God accomplished His purposes through him. Though they did not heed His message, they did know God had spoken to them through Amos.

God also called and used Jeremiah in a similar way. Though the pattern is very similar, the messenger is different. Listen to what happened:

> *Then the word of the Lord came to me, saying: "Before I formed you in the womb I knew you; Before you were born I sanctified you; I ordained you a prophet to the nations." Then said I: "Ah, Lord GOD! Behold, I cannot speak, for I am a youth." But the LORD said to me: "Do not say, 'I am a youth,' for you shall go to all to whom I send you, and whatever I command you, you shall speak. Do not be afraid of their faces, for I am with you to deliver you," says the LORD. Then the LORD put forth His hand and touched my mouth, and the LORD said to me: "Behold, I have put My words in your mouth. See, I have this day set you over the nations and over the kingdoms, to root out and to pull down, to destroy and to throw down, to build and to plant." Moreover the word of the LORD came to me, saying, "Jeremiah, what do you see?" And I said, "I see a branch of an almond tree." Then the LORD said to me, "You have seen well, for I am ready to perform My word."*
>
> JEREMIAH 1:4–12 (NKJV)

God would speak clearly and forcefully to His people, Judah and Jerusalem, and He chose Jeremiah. But the heart of God knew long before Jeremiah was even born that He had "set him apart" for this important time in history. This time was critical for His people. God wanted both a long and a passionate pleading from His heart to come to His people. Jeremiah was then shaped by God to be the one through whom He would speak. So tender was the message to Judah that Jeremiah was called "the weeping prophet"!

They did not listen, either. The temple, the city of Jerusalem, and all the towns and villages of Judah were destroyed. Many were killed and the most skilled of the land were taken into captivity in Babylon—for seventy years.

God has found messengers through whom He could speak and work in every generation in history. Some of the most significant include Moses (Exodus 3:15), the judges, David, all the prophets, the disciples, the apostle Paul, and God's people throughout history. This God-chosen process continues to this very day and is the way God will call and work through your life, too. God has worked and moved throughout history to accomplish His eternal purpose. Always, eternity is in the balance. Those He chooses, calls, shapes, and uses are painfully and deeply aware of "this assignment." They are the clay and God is the potter. God always has a design in mind when He chooses a person (read Jeremiah 18:1–6).

Read Jeremiah 18:1-6. Then explain how God is shaping your life.

Moreover God said to Moses, "Thus you shall say to the children of Israel: 'The LORD God of your fathers, the God of Abraham, the God of Isaac, and the God of Jacob, has sent me to you. This is My name forever, and this is My memorial to all generations.'"
EXODUS 3:15

UNIT 5 CALLED & ACCOUNTABLE

_____

_____

_____

_____

_____

_____

_____

_____

THOUGHT FOR THE DAY

THOSE GOD CHOOSES AND CALLS KNOW IT IS GOD, KNOW WHAT HE IS SAYING, AND KNOW HOW THEY ARE TO RELEASE THEIR LIVES TO HIM FOR HIS PURPOSES IN THEIR DAY!

What assignment are you deeply aware of that God has given you in the last month?

_____

_____

_____

_____

_____

_____

_____

_____

_____

DAY 2
A DAILY WALK, THOROUGHLY REARRANGED

When God sees a growing, loving, and responsive relationship of trust in Him by one of His children, He continues His call on that person's life. He usually does this in the midst of a person's daily routine. Through this daily routine, God calls a person to a special and deeper relationship with Him. It is also remarkable that the daily response of each person brings the enabling presence and power of the Spirit of God closer to being accomplished through a person's assignment with God.

For example, God placed His Spirit on the responsive Moses, and later on the seventy elders who were to work with him (read Numbers 11:16–25). The daily walk of Moses with God, guiding His people, was exceedingly demanding for Moses. It would require the full presence and enabling that only the Spirit of God could bring. But God also provided seventy other key leaders who would share his load of leadership. They would require the same Spirit of God. God provided thoroughly, and certainly adequately, for them all. This enabling provided what was needed for the leaders to guide God's people according to His commands and purposes.

Who has God put alongside your life to help you share your load of leadership? How does God use them to help you?

Later, God commanded Moses to build a tabernacle for His presence among His people. It would require the utmost care and obedience to all God would direct. God told Moses He had already chosen and placed His Spirit on some men who would do all that He commanded (read Exodus 35:30–36:21). They were ordinary workmen, chosen by God and equipped by God's Spirit to do His will in all things.

This pattern of God working through ordinary people, called, assigned, and enabled by God, continued through each of the judges of Israel. Each was called at a crucial moment in the life of God's people when they needed deliverance from their enemies. David's life follows this same pattern (read 1 Samuel 16:13); the disciples and the apostle Paul also were shaped and used by God in their day.

Now it is our turn. This is especially true because God has huge purposes to accomplish through His people in our day. Our world is changing, and God is orchestrating His people for His purposes. But oftentimes they are not in a spiritual condition to respond to Him! So once again, God is looking for someone who will "*stand in the gap before Me on behalf of the land, that I should not destroy it*" (Ezekiel 22:30).

GOD HAS HUGE PURPOSES TO ACCOMPLISH THROUGH HIS PEOPLE IN OUR DAY. OUR WORLD IS CHANGING, AND GOD IS ORCHESTRATING HIS PEOPLE FOR HIS PURPOSES.

So much is in the balance, especially eternally. The heart of God has not changed. He is not willing that any should perish, but that all should come to repentance (2 Peter 3:9). So in this our day, and in your life and mine, it is still incredibly true:

> *For the eyes of the Lord run to and fro throughout the whole earth, to show Himself strong on behalf of those whose heart is loyal to Him.*
> 2 CHRONICLES 16:9 (NKJV)

So the process continues. But now it involves you, and it involves me! And God is watching to see how we will respond to Him.

THOUGHT FOR THE DAY

GOD KNOWS THE SPIRITUAL CONDITION OF EVERY HEART, AND KNOWS THE KIND AND QUALITY OF RESPONSE THAT WILL BE GIVEN TO HIM. HE CHOOSES LIVES WHOSE HEARTS ARE COMPLETE IN EVERY WAY TOWARD HIM.

In what ways does the spiritual condition of your heart show that you are becoming "complete" in your relationship with Him?

DAY 3
COMPLETELY ENABLED

As already mentioned, the one God calls, He also thoroughly and completely equips to enable them to respond in every matter toward God. God is on mission. The servant of the Lord must "be where the Master is." And Jesus added significantly, *"If anyone serves Me, the Father will honor him"* (John 12:26). Whole books could be written just on this intimate relationship between the Lord and His servants. But the enabling provision of God for His servants is clearly declared and seen throughout Scripture and history. Some of the "provisions of God" are clear:

> **And my God will supply all your needs according to His riches in glory in Christ Jesus.**
> PHILIPPIANS 4:19 (HCSB)

GOD IS ON MISSION.

For every one of God's promises is "Yes" in Him. Therefore the "Amen" is also through Him for God's glory through us.
2 CORINTHIANS 1:20 (HCSB)

For His divine power has given us everything required for life and godliness, through the knowledge of Him who called us by His own glory and goodness. By these He has given us very great and precious promises, so that through them you may share in the divine nature, escaping the corruption that is in the world because of evil desires.
2 PETER 1:3–4 (HCSB)

But the greatest of God's provisions is His Holy Spirit. Jesus assured His disciples, "*you will receive power when the Holy Spirit has come upon you*" (Acts 1:8). He had earlier assured them, "*And I will ask the Father, and He will give you another Counselor to be with you forever. He is the Spirit of truth*" (John 14:16–17*a*).

The Holy Spirit is God Himself, present and active, enabling every believer to do whatever God commanded. He would always let them know the Father's will for each of them (John 16:13; 1 Corinthians 2:9–16). He would guide them into all truth, teach them all things, and bring to their remembrance everything Christ had commanded them (John 14:26; John 16:13–15). He would also help them when they prayed (Romans 8:26), something that would be so much a part of their relationship to God and His will in their lives.

And the Holy Spirit would work the Scriptures into their lives as a "sword" (Ephesians 6:17).

Those God used in the Old Testament had the Spirit come upon them to totally enable them. In the New Testament, every believer would have the Spirit of God at conversion. But more significantly, the Holy Spirit would "fill" those whom God called to be available to Him as He took His great salvation message to the whole world.

Now it is our turn. And all that was available to people in Scripture is available today to every believer called of God. No matter what it is that God commands the believer to do with Him, His provision is already present and available, and the Holy Spirit is actively working to implement all of it into that believer's life. No matter how "difficult or impossible" an assignment God places on the life of one of His children, God's provision will completely enable them to do it.

ALL THAT WAS AVAILABLE TO PEOPLE IN SCRIPTURE IS AVAILABLE TODAY TO EVERY BELIEVER CALLED OF GOD.

God's provision for every believer on mission with God is the fullness of His presence. In His presence we are "complete" (Colossians 2:9–10). Every believer is enabled to experience God finishing His work through them (read Philippians 1:6). The Holy Spirit does this in many ways.

One way of enabling comes as the believer spends time in God's Word. In the midst of the study, the Holy Spirit gives a confirming "Yes" to what He knows to be the will of God. It comes as a quiet assurance, giving peace and joy. He also gives affirmation when the believer takes time to pray and seek assurance from God of His will. To the carefully observant person who prays, there comes a quiet direction to the prayer, putting the person into the center of the will of God (read Romans 8:26–28). When John was praying on the island of Patmos, the Holy Spirit gave him clear direction concerning the will of God (read Revelation 1).

What affirmations has God brought to you in your last seven days of prayer?

_____

_____

_____

_____

_____

_____

_____

Throughout history, the witness of those used of God indicates that some of the great affirmations of God have come to them in prayer. Further affirmations of God come by what He is doing around the believer, and in the midst of His people, the local church.

It is important to keep in mind that God can and does affirm His will for His servants. If God does *not* express Himself toward you, He may be trying to let you know something else. When God promises something, He does it. If you sense you know God's will, and yet do not see God doing what He promised, God may be seeking to tell you that either you are not in His will (read Isaiah 46:11*b*; Isaiah 14:24, 27;

IF YOU SENSE YOU KNOW GOD'S WILL, AND YET DO NOT SEE GOD DOING WHAT HE PROMISED, GOD MAY BE SEEKING TO TELL YOU THAT EITHER YOU ARE NOT IN HIS WILL OR THAT HIS TIMING IS NOT ALWAYS IMMEDIATE.

1 Kings 8:56) or that His timing is not always immediate. God may be taking the time necessary to develop character in your life before He can give you all He has planned for you. Ask God and He will guide you to know the truth of your situation.

THOUGHT FOR THE DAY

GOD HAS PROMISED INCREDIBLE AFFIRMATION OF HIS WILL AND HIS CALL IN OUR LIVES. IT IS IMPORTANT THAT EACH BELIEVER BE CONSTANTLY ALERT TO GOD'S WORD OF CONFIRMATION, HOWEVER HE CHOOSES TO EXPRESS IT. BUT NEVER GO LONG WITHOUT SOME AFFIRMATION FROM THE LORD THAT YOU ARE IN THE CENTER OF HIS WILL.

Describe the evidence of the activity of God in your life concerning the last assignment God placed in your life:

Day 4
Necessity of Functioning In the Body

Christians will also more completely know when they are being *called* by God as they function in the life of His church (the body of Christ). The most complete pictures of the body working together are found in 1 Corinthians 12, Ephesians 4, and Romans 12. Each member in the body functions where God places him or her in the body, and each assists the other parts of the body to grow up into the Head, which is Christ. This is not merely a figure of speech; it is a living reality. The loving Christ is truly present in the church body, and each member really does assist the others to know and do the will of God. Paul constantly affirmed his need of other believers to help him know and carry out the call of God in his life.

> *For I want very much to see you, that I may impart to you some spiritual gift to strengthen you, that is, to be mutually encouraged by each other's faith, both yours and mine.*
>
> Romans 1:11–12 (HCSB)

> *Pray also for me, that the message may be given to me when I open my mouth to make known with boldness the mystery of the gospel. For this I am an ambassador in chains. Pray that I might be bold enough in Him to speak as I should.*
>
> Ephesians 6:19–20 (HCSB)

In the church where God places you He has provided other believers whom He has equipped to assist you in:

Knowing God's call and activity in your life,

and whom God has chosen to:

Assist you in carrying out His will.

Your life in the body of Christ is crucial if God is to carry out His eternal purpose for your life today. The eye can assist the ear to know what it is hearing, the hand as to what it is feeling, and the feet where to step next. The life of the body is affected by each member relating in love to one another (Ephesians 4:16).

YOUR LIFE IN THE BODY OF CHRIST IS CRUCIAL IF GOD IS TO CARRY OUT HIS ETERNAL PURPOSE FOR YOUR LIFE TODAY.

Read Ephesians 4:1–16. How does God use you in the life of the body?

This will involve you not only in your church family but also with the other churches in your local area (as happened in the New Testament), across the nation, and around the world. God's call is to take the gospel to every person and into every nation. God's plan for accomplishing this is to call you to Himself, and then place your life alongside all the others He has called, so that together as one people He can work dramatically across an entire world through you and through His people!

THOUGHT FOR THE DAY

GOD'S CALL IN YOUR LIFE ALWAYS INCLUDES YOUR INTIMATE INVOLVEMENT WITH HIS PEOPLE IN AND THROUGH YOUR LOCAL CHURCH.

What have you discovered is the reason God placed you in the local church where you are a member?

Day 5
Full Affirmation

In a personal relationship with God, God in love affirms His presence and His call in your life daily! The heart that seeks Him, finds Him; the life that asks Him, receives; to the one who knocks, God opens a door (Matthew 7:7–11). God responds to His children, and they know that it is God who is affirming their relationship with Him.

The heart (life) that is earnestly seeking Him will daily spend time in God's Word. When we do, the Holy Spirit uses the Word of God like a sword (Ephesians 6:17) to convict us of sin, to lead us into "all truth," to teach us "all things," to bring to our remembrance all that Christ has been saying to us, and to help us thoroughly understand and apply His will and call to our lives (read John 14:26; John 16:7–15).

As a believer opens the Scripture, the Holy Spirit is present and actively seeking to bring the earnest seeker into the will of God. Words have sudden new meanings and seem to apply directly to our life—and they really do, for this is the affirmation of God in our life through the working of the Holy Spirit. The same is true of all Scripture, in particular the life and teachings of Jesus. But *"all Scripture is inspired by God and is profitable for teaching, for rebuking, for correcting, for training in righteousness,"* (2 Timothy 3:16)—especially under the ministry of the Holy Spirit. Throughout the entire process, the Holy Spirit keeps "bearing witness with our spirit," not only that we are children of God, but that we are in the center of the will of God (Romans 8:16, 27).

What has God shown you in the Scriptures this week that has sudden new meaning for you?

The person with a heart seeking after God will also spend much time in prayer. God has given the Holy Spirit the responsibility to guide each of us into the will of God as we pray (Romans 8:26–27). Too often, our prayer begins quite self-centered and self-focused! As we continue to pray, soon our prayer turns to God-centeredness. This is the Holy Spirit at work, according to the will of God. Follow the Spirit's directives immediately and completely.

You may be praying with anger, even resentment against someone or some situation. Soon God's love fills your heart, and your prayer changes to expressions of love and blessing. This is God. He has affirmed not only His presence but also His will toward your life. Thank Him and alter everything into His directives, for He is ready to bless you greatly!

Sometimes God uses friends, or family, or persons in your church to give you affirmation for your call. Someone shares a Scripture with you that is the very same Scripture

God gave you that morning. This is God's affirmation! A timely phone call or letter comes. Again, God's affirmation to your life and call. A caution, or even a word of correction becomes God's affirmation *not* to proceed.

Remember, there are no coincidences in the life wholly yielded to God! God is wholly involved in the life of the one He calls to go with Him. But there is an additional word to share at this point. If you see NO affirming presence of God in your life or ministry, you need to stop and see if indeed you may be out of God's will, and He is speaking to you by *not* giving affirmation to your sin and rebellion or disobedience. It is also important to remember that "success" as the world defines it may not at all be the affirming presence of God.

THERE ARE NO COINCIDENCES IN THE LIFE WHOLLY YIELDED TO GOD! GOD IS WHOLLY INVOLVED IN THE LIFE OF THE ONE HE CALLS TO GO WITH HIM.

THOUGHT FOR THE DAY

GOD NEVER LEAVES HIS CHILDREN TO GUESS WHETHER THEY ARE WALKING IN THE CENTER OF HIS WILL. HE PROVIDES PLENTY OF DAILY ASSURANCES!

What "full affirmation" is God placing in your life presently?

Called & Accountable
Mary Slessor

"Anywhere Provided It Be Forward"

Duke Town in Calabar, West Africa, was called the "White Man's Graveyard." It was a gateway to some of the most barbaric places in Africa where witchcraft, superstition, cannibalism, and human sacrifice were part of everyday life. It was home to malaria and other deadly jungle diseases. All of this Mary Slessor faced when she arrived from Scotland in 1876, at 28 years of age, with a determination to tell the people of Calabar of her Savior Jesus Christ.

From an early age, Mary had dreamed of going to Africa as a missionary for her Lord. Upon arriving in Duke Town (which is now part of southeast Nigeria), Mary quickly learned the language of the people and began to venture out into the surrounding area. She traveled alone, knowing the dangers of doing so, but felt compelled to tell the people of Calabar about Jesus Christ.

Mary lived as the African people lived and gave herself to caring for those she encountered. She urged them to forsake their barbaric practices, treated and cared for the sick, took in orphans, and settled disputes. She taught them about the one true God and encouraged them to forsake the evil spirits and many "gods" that they worshiped. As she began to see some fruit from her labors, Mary desired to move on, "anywhere provided it be forward," so that others could hear the good news of Jesus Christ.

Though she faced tremendous dangers from the people she sought to reach and suffered greatly from fevers, boils, and other illnesses, Mary continued to move farther into the interior of Africa. When she became too feeble to walk, she was pulled by cart from village to village, always advancing into the unknown so the unreached could hear about Jesus Christ.

In 1915, thirty-five years after her arrival in Calabar, Mary Slessor succumbed to the diseases she often battled. Yet because she had been willing to go anywhere, hundreds upon hundreds had been set free by Jesus Christ.

CALLED & ACCOUNTABLE

UNIT 6

HOW DO I LIVE OUT THE CALL?

UNIT 6

HOW DO I LIVE OUT THE CALL?

ESSENTIAL TRUTH FOR THE WEEK

God's provisions for a relationship with Him are completely thorough. Nothing is missing from God's perspective. What would it take to miss His calling? You would have to resist, quench, and grieve Him, His Son, and His Holy Spirit to miss His call.

CALLED & ACCOUNTABLE
BETH MOORE

LIVING PROOF

Beth Moore is a well-known Christian author and conference speaker. Her resources have helped thousands of women be set free by Jesus Christ. To read her books and to hear her speak is to know that God has called and equipped Beth to teach people to love and live out God's Word. Yet while she knew that God had called her, it took time for Beth to discover how God wanted to use her.

Beth Moore knew God was calling her to serve Him when she was an 18-year-old camp counselor. A cabin full of sixth-graders at a missions camp may not sound like an environment where God would speak, but it was at such a place that God clearly revealed to Beth that He wanted her life for His purposes. Beth yielded her life willingly and totally to the God she had known since childhood.

Immediately, Beth sought to discover how God wanted her to serve Him. She felt that God called women to sing, play an instrument, or be a missionary, and she was willing to be any of those. However, Beth knew that her musical abilities were limited, and God did not seem to be asking her to serve as a missionary. What did God want her to do?

Though unclear about how God would use her, Beth was clear that God was calling her. She continued to be open to God's direction and decided to follow God one step at a time. Following God led her to a college education, marriage, two children, and lots of life experiences. God also directed her to a wonderful church, where her pastor and others helped Beth to understand how God wanted to use her. Beth made monumental mistakes along the way, and even expected God to revoke her calling. But God was faithful to redeem and to birth in her a passion for His Word. Step by step, God prepared and equipped Beth to be a vessel He could use to affect the lives of many people.

Today, Beth's life and ministry are living proof that when God calls us to Himself, He is faithful to prepare and equip us to fit into His perfect plan to touch our world.

Day 1
Desire to Follow The Call

God Himself places within the heart of every believer the deepest desire to experience the strong presence and power of God working in him and through him. God will not override your heart or your will, but He will thoroughly influence your life toward His will and His call. Notice this in this Scripture passage:

> *So then, my dear friends, just as you have always obeyed, not only in my presence, but now even more in my absence, work out your own salvation with fear and trembling. For it is God who is working among you both the willing and the working for His good purpose.*
>
> Philippians 2:12–13 (HCSB)

But how, from the Scriptural revelation, does one come to experience in life the deep reality of being called and accountable?

As we look for the answer to this question, it is important to remember that not only is it

1. *"God who is working among you both the willing and the working for His good purpose"* (Philippians 2:13)

but also,

2. *"He who started a good work in you will carry it on to completion until the day of Christ Jesus"* (Philippians 1:6).

These two truths carry with them enormous implications!

Look up Ephesians 3:20–21 and 2 Peter 1:1–11. Write your reflections below.

THOUGHT FOR THE DAY

THE INNER DESIRE TO KNOW GOD'S CALL AND TO COM-
PLETELY DO IT IS GRANTED TO EVERY BELIEVER.

But how, from the Scriptural revelation, does one come to experience in life the deep reality of being called and accountable?

Write how you would answer this question and then discuss your answer with other Christians.

Day 2
The Activity of God

First, when you are a Christian living in the world, God is actively at work in your life the moment you begin to sense an inner desire to do the will of God. God's timing for your full response is in place! This is the activity of God in your life causing you to want to do His will. The activity of God may be experienced while you are studying the Bible, or when you are worshiping in your church, or when you are praying, or in the midst of your daily routine, or even when you are talking with a friend or one of your family. There are some things that only God can do. Creating awareness of His call is something only God can do in a believer's life.

Here are a few examples.

There are some things that only God can do.

Bill and Anne responded very differently than other people when the community learned that a policeman in our city had been murdered. The two young men who committed the crime were arrested, and the anger of the people in the city mounted. But during our prayer meeting, Bill and Anne began to weep as they shared a deep burden in their hearts for the parents of the two young men arrested. They themselves had a son in jail, and they knew the pain and loneliness of being the parents. As they shared their hearts, the entire church family began to understand and feel their pain too. We knew God was trying to speak to us through them.

Bill and Anne asked that we pray for them because they had invited the parents of these two boys to their home for coffee. They had also told the parents of their concern and God's personal love and concern. We did agree to pray.

The parents of the two boys cried out, "We have been hated and cursed by others. You are the only persons who have cared about our hurt. Thank you!"

Out of this experience, our church family, along with Bill and Anne, began an extensive jail ministry—to both the inmates and the parents and family in several jails and prisons. The entire church became involved. Why? Because two believers knew they were children of a loving God and knew that God was calling them to respond. God wanted to work through them and their church in the lives of others who were hurting. One of our mission churches was even begun with families of prison inmates.

Another woman, Cathy, joined our church. The prayer meeting became a very special place for her. In the meetings, as she prayed, she often sensed the moving of God in her life, giving her clear direction.

One Wednesday evening she shared, "God has given me a great burden for ministering to the mentally and physically disadvantaged and their families. I grew up with a mentally handicapped sister. I know what this does to the parents and the family. No one in the churches of our city is ministering to these people. I sense we should seek God's guidance to see if we should be involved." The more she shared and the more we prayed, the more our hearts came together as one (read Matthew 18:19–20).

Read Matthew 18:19-20. Give an illustration from your life of how God has brought two people together for prayer.

Again I assure you: If two of you on earth agree about any matter that you pray for, it will be done for you by My Father in heaven. For where two or three are gathered together in My name, I am there among them.
MATTHEW 18:19–20

_____

_____

_____

_____

_____

_____

_____

We became convinced that God was directing not only Cathy but also our entire church to become involved. To us it was a clear call of God, and we felt accountable to God to respond. We did, and Cathy helped us know what to do. Soon we had 15 to 20 mentally limited young adults attending church with us, and some of their family members. Our church came to experience more of the meaning of pure love through these special people than we had ever experienced before. God called Cathy and her church as she prayed (and then we prayed with her), and God began to accomplish His loving purposes through us.

THOUGHT FOR THE DAY

GOD WILL NOT LET YOU "MISS" HIS CALL ON YOUR LIFE OR YOUR CHURCH WHEN YOU ARE INTENTLY LISTENING IN AN ABIDING FELLOWSHIP WITH HIM!

Write a story that shares the current activity of God in your church.

DAY 3
CORPORATE CALLING

Terry worked in a very significant microchip company. As he studied his Bible, prayed, and worshiped regularly, God began to speak to him. During a worship service, Terry came forward indicating that God was calling him to be a more effective witness in his place of work.

"But," he said, "my desk is out of the way at the end of a hall and only one person comes by my office. How can God use me to witness to the many in my office?"

I shared his sense of call with the church, and we pledged to pray with him. I encouraged him to look carefully for the activity of God in answer to our prayer and to be prepared to obey immediately. It was not long before he joyfully shared with the church: "This week my boss came to me and said, 'Terry, I want to move your desk. I hope you don't mind!' My desk now is in the busiest place in the office, right at the drinking fountain, the copier, and the coffee center. Everybody comes by my desk now. Please pray for me that I will be the faithful witness God has called me to be in my workplace!"

This experience caused the entire church to be more sensitive to God's call in their life, as well as to the church.

Many significant purposes of God were worked out over the next year. A car mechanic (who is from the Philippines) and his wife clearly sensed God was calling them into full-time ministry. They believed God wanted them to pastor the thousands of Filipino families in our city and our nation. I encouraged and counseled them from the Scriptures while their church family prayed for them. They responded to let God work through them. He has finished his seminary training, has been pastoring an influential Filipino church, and has led the church to start two new mission churches. He has sensed the call of God now to include establishing such churches across the entire nation (Canada).

The church also began an outreach to refugees arriving without documentation from nations around the world. Many have been saved and a high percentage have sensed God saved them physically, and now spiritually and eternally. They now believe God would have them minister the gospel to "their people," some even returning to their native land.

THOUGHT FOR THE DAY

THE LOCAL CHURCH IS CRUCIAL FOR EVERY BELIEVER IN BEING CALLED AND BEING ACCOUNTABLE TO GOD FOR THEIR CALLING.

How would you describe "corporate calling?"

Find a few Biblical examples of "corporate calling" and list the references here.

_____

_____

_____

_____

DAY 4
DAILY LIVING

How do you live out the call of God in your life? It begins and is sustained in your daily relationship with God, from the beginning of the day to the end of the day! In your quiet time alone with God at the beginning of the day, God speaks to you and guides you to understand and know what He is planning to do that day through where He has your life.

If you close this time by saying, "O God, please go with me this day and bless me!" God may say to you, "You have it backwards! I have a will and plan for what I want to do through your life today. I want you to go with Me. So I am alerting you now through My word and your praying to know My will for you, so you can be partners with Me today!"

In your same quiet time, the Lord Jesus will bring to your heart the full assurance that whatever the Father has in mind, He (Jesus) will be present with you and in you to provide all the resources you will need to see the Father's will fulfilled through you. In addition to that, the Holy Spirit will be giving

His assurance that He will enable you to implement in your life this specific will of God, and any call of God! What an incredible privilege! What an awesome responsibility! What an accountability we have to love Him, believe Him, trust Him, and obey Him. It is then that you will experience the wonderful presence and power of God working His will in you and through you.

Second, because you know that God is working in you and will complete what He has begun, you should live with a clear sense of expectation and anticipation of God's doing this in your life daily. It is not what you can do for God, but what God is doing in you! And what He begins, He Himself will bring to completion.

How encouraging it is to read again in Isaiah a further promise from God:

> *The Lord of hosts has sworn, saying, "Surely, as I have thought, so it shall come to pass, and as I have purposed, so it shall stand. For the Lord of hosts has purposed, and who will annul it? His hand is stretched out, and who will turn it back?"*
> Isaiah 14:24, 27 (NKJV)

Once God has spoken to your heart, it is as good as done. For God has never spoken to reveal His will and not Himself guaranteed the completion of what He has said. This will be as true for you as for anyone in the Bible or history.

Study for yourself the following additional Scripture passages to give yourself further encouragement: Isaiah 55:8; Numbers 23:19; Hebrews 13:20–21.

IT IS NOT WHAT YOU CAN DO FOR GOD, BUT WHAT GOD IS DOING IN YOU!

GOD HAS NEVER SPOKEN TO REVEAL HIS WILL AND NOT HIMSELF GUARANTEED THE COMPLETION OF WHAT HE HAS SAID.

Study Isaiah 55:8; Numbers 23:19; Hebrews 13:20-21.
What encouragement did these Scriptures give to you?

_____

_____

_____

_____

_____

Third, it will be important to recognize the activity or working of God in your life so you can quickly join Him. Jesus made this very clear in His own relationship with the Father when He said:

> *"My Father is still working, and I also am working."*
> *. . . Then Jesus replied, "I assure you: The Son is not*
> *able to do anything on His own, but only what He*
> *sees the Father doing. For whatever the Father does,*
> *these things the Son also does in the same way. For*
> *the Father loves the Son and shows Him everything*
> *He is doing, and He will show Him greater works*
> *than these so that you will be amazed."*
> JOHN 5:17, 19–20 (HCSB)

In John 6:44, 45, 65, Jesus said that no one would come to Him unless the Father drew and taught them. But those in whose life the Father was working would come to Him. Jesus, therefore, would look for such drawing in the lives of those around Him. For instance, when He saw Zacchaeus up a tree,

He might have said to Himself, "No one could seek after Me with that kind of earnestness unless My Father was at work in his life. I've got to join My Father's activity." So he left the crowd and went to Zacchaeus' house, and salvation came to Zacchaeus that night!

Sherri, a nurse at our university, asked the church to pray that God would help her witness to others. But she did not know just where. I, as her pastor, shared these Scripture passages with her and encouraged her to look for the "activity of God—things only God could do" that were happening around her life, and then be ready to let her life be available for God to use. She came back to the church excited, saying, "A girl who has been in classes with me for two years came up to me and said, 'I think you might be a Christian. I need to talk to you.' I joined her, and she said, 'Eleven of us girls are trying to study the Bible, but none of us is a Christian. Do you know someone who could teach us the Bible?'"

From this contact, Sherri became involved in the lives of many college students in Bible study and witness, and a number became Christians and united with our church.

Think back on your life over the past week or month. Let the Holy Spirit bring to your remembrance how God has been speaking clearly to you. Now that you have a fresh understanding of this from this study:

1. List in the margin the ways God has been speaking to you.

2. Be freshly committed to watch and respond to God in those activities.

3. Share with your church and see if God would include them, too.

THOUGHT FOR THE DAY

TWENTY-FOUR HOURS A DAY, GOD CAN AND WILL SPEAK TO YOU ABOUT WHAT HE IS PURPOSING TO ACCOMPLISH THROUGH YOU. BE ALERT ALL DAY AND ALL NIGHT FOR HIS VOICE.

How are you recognizing the Father's activity in your life and in your church?

_____

_____

_____

_____

_____

_____

_____

_____

DAY 5
INTERDEPENDENCE

When God alerts you to where He is working, He intends for you to become involved with Him so He can accomplish His will for others through your life.

But there is a further truth about applying, or living out, God's call in your life and responding to Him with sincere accountability. That is your **interdependence** with other believers in the life of your church. Not only will they help you to know and clarify the will of God, or the call of God, in your life, but they will also stand alongside you to assist you in fulfilling it. It is what I call divine interdependence. There are no loners in the living of the Christian life. We are mutually dependent upon each other. The New Testament describes this interdependence in the Christian life as life in the body of Christ.

Three major Scripture passages help us to understand this clearly: Romans 12:3–8; 1 Corinthians 12:4–31; Ephesians 4:1–7, 11–16.

Read Romans 12:3-8; 1 Corinthians 12:4-31; Ephesians 4:1-7, 11-16. How do these passages help you understand interdependence?

Paul strongly reminds the believers that they need each other, just as a body needs every part. He said, *"And those parts of the body that we think to be less honorable, we clothe these with greater honor, and our unpresentable parts have a better presentation"* (1 Corinthians 12:23). And in Ephesians 4:13 he reminds them that when each part in the body functions effectively where God has placed them, then the entire body grows up into the Head, which is Christ, *"until we all reach unity in the faith and in the knowledge of God's Son, growing into a mature man with a stature measured by Christ's fullness."*

This will call for a joyful, willing **accountability** each to the other because we are all united to the Head, Jesus Christ. This is by divine plan. God would call us to Himself, but He would also with that call unite us with other believers in mutual love and accountability for the well being of each other. In the church, we encourage each believer to anticipate that God would

1. Work out their salvation call.
2. Take them on mission with Himself and others in their world.

Expectation and anticipation become a way of life, and we are not disappointed.

In the church, we experience together the excitement of being on mission. Ministry to the down-and-out, to the school system, to the jails, to the mentally and physically handicapped, to the university, to the Indian reservations, to the surrounding towns and villages, and even to the ends of the earth was experienced by the members of our church.

Everyone became involved, individually and together, with God. Many felt called to be pastors or church staff; others felt called to minister in other countries of the world; still others gained a clear sense of a call to serve, witness, and minister in the marketplace and the homes where God had placed them. Together we helped each other to be **accountable**— first to God who had called us and then to each other as we sought to be a body of Christ in our world through which the Father could and would carry out His purposes.

To "Be Accountable" includes:

1. Believing what God has said and revealed in His Word. Every one God had called, He held accountable to answer to Him specifically. He also holds us accountable before Him.
2. Being immediately obedient to all God speaks, with "fear and trembling" (Philippians 2:12).
3. Choosing a spiritual partner, or class, or entire church, to hold you accountable to *do* what you know God has said.
4. Taking spiritual inventory frequently, looking for clear evidence of God's activity and blessing through you.
5. Being aware of an ultimate eternal moment before God for your "works" done in this life (2 Corinthians 5:10).

THOUGHT FOR THE DAY

ONE OF GOD'S GREATEST PROVISIONS FOR YOU IS TO ASSURE YOU OF HIS WILL.

CONCLUSION

The call of God is a call to a total relationship with God for the purposes He had for us from before the foundation of the world. God calls us by causing us to want to do His will and then enabling us to do it. He first calls each of us to be His child by faith in Jesus, His Son. In that relationship, God has provided all we need to live fully with Him. That relationship will always involve us in His redemptive activity in our world. In that relationship, God Himself will work through us in our world. As God works through us in our world, we will come to know Him and grow toward Christlikeness. A Christlike character is God's preparation for eternity with Him. What a plan and what a purpose God has for each of us! May we respond to Him as He works in us and through us mightily in our world.

Called and Accountable—God's greatest of privileges given freely to every believer!

CALLED & ACCOUNTABLE

LEADER'S GUIDE

GOD'S PURPOSE FOR EVERY BELIEVER

How to Use this Leader's Guide

If you are leading *Called & Accountable* as a group study, this Leader's Guide will help you plan for group meetings. These two pages provide generic guidelines; refer to them when using the planning pages for each unit, found on pp. 148-159.

Before Each Session

1. Complete all five days of the unit during your daily quiet times.

2. Pray, asking the Spirit's guidance for the session. Be right with God, confessing any known sin, so you may be a pure vessel for Him to use, excited to share truth. Pray for each group member.

3. Study each section with the magnifying glass icon. Identify from this section a few points for group discussion.

4. Prepare specifics for leading the session by filling in the "During the Session" page for the unit (see Planning Pages, pp. 148–159).

5. Attend to any logistical issues, such as arranging the meeting place, posting signs, planning for refreshments, contacting group members, or gathering needed materials.

6. Make your own checklist in the space provided for you.

DURING EACH SESSION

1. Welcome and Prayer: Plan to welcome members and open with a short time of prayer. As group members become closer, allow time for sharing prayer requests before prayer.

2. Questions/Insights from Testimonies: Plan questions or comments for a brief discussion of the *Called & Accountable* testimonies for the week, found at the beginning and end of each unit. (Unit 6 has one testimony and a conclusion.) Possible questions: How did you respond to the testimonies? What was unusual about them? Has God ever called you in such a way?

3. Major Truths of Study: Plan to bring out the main truths of the unit by reviewing and discussing the Essential Truth for the Week, the Thoughts for the Day, and the sections with the magnifying glass icons.

4. Discussion Questions Drawn from Study: Develop questions to lead the group to listen to what God is teaching them through their study. Focus on creating readiness for learning, reinforcing important truths, and stimulating personal application. Possible questions:
- What did God say to you as you studied this unit?
- What were some statements in the workbook that were particularly important to you?
- What adjustments is God asking you to make?

5. Summary/Challenge: Summarize the important learning that was experienced by the group in this session. Challenge them to be diligent in completing the daily studies and in praying.

6. Create Anticipation: Prepare the group for the next session by creating anticipation for the new unit.

7. Prayer: Pray for the group before they leave, using Scriptures and their applications from the group discussion.

WELCOME
AND PRAYER
(10 minutes)

TESTIMONIES
(5 minutes)

TRUTHS
(10 minutes)

QUESTIONS
(15 minutes)

SUMMARY &
CHALLENGE
(5 minutes)

NEXT WEEK
(5 minutes)

PRAYER
(10 minutes)

PLANNING PAGES FOR UNIT ONE

BEFORE THE SESSION

1. Complete all five days of the unit during your daily quiet times.

2. Pray, asking the Spirit's guidance for the session. Be right with God, confessing any known sin, so you may be a pure vessel for Him to use, excited to share truth. Pray for each group member.

3. Study each section with the magnifying glass icon. Identify from this section a few points for group discussion.

4. Prepare specifics for leading the session by filling in the "During the Session" page for the unit at right. Adapt the suggested segments to your group's needs.

5. Attend to any logistical issues, such as arranging the meeting place, posting signs, planning for refreshments, contacting group members, or gathering needed materials.

6. Make your own checklist:

DURING THE SESSION

(Refer to page 147 for suggestions for using this page)

1. Welcome/Prayer:

    Prayer Requests:

WELCOME
AND PRAYER
(10 minutes)

2. Questions/Insights from Testimonies:

TESTIMONIES
(5 minutes)

3. Major Truths of Study:

TRUTHS
(10 minutes)

4. Discussion Questions Drawn from Study:

QUESTIONS
(15 minutes)

5. Summary/Challenge:

SUMMARY &
CHALLENGE
(5 minutes)

6. Create Anticipation:

NEXT WEEK
(5 minutes)

7. Prayer:

PRAYER
(10 minutes)

PLANNING PAGES FOR UNIT TWO

BEFORE THE SESSION

1. Complete all five days of the unit during your daily quiet times.

2. Pray, asking the Spirit's guidance for the session. Be right with God, confessing any known sin, so you may be a pure vessel for Him to use, excited to share truth. Pray for each group member.

3. Study each section with the magnifying glass icon. Identify from this section a few points for group discussion.

4. Prepare specifics for leading the session by filling in the "During the Session" page for the unit at right. Adapt the suggested segments to your group's needs.

5. Attend to any logistical issues, such as arranging the meeting place, posting signs, planning for refreshments, contacting group members, or gathering needed materials.

6. Make your own checklist:

DURING THE SESSION

(Refer to page 147 for suggestions for using this page)

1. **Welcome/Prayer:**

   Prayer Requests:

WELCOME
AND PRAYER
(10 minutes)

2. **Questions/Insights from Testimonies:**

TESTIMONIES
(5 minutes)

3. **Major Truths of Study:**

TRUTHS
(10 minutes)

4. **Discussion Questions Drawn from Study:**

QUESTIONS
(15 minutes)

5. **Summary/Challenge:**

SUMMARY &
CHALLENGE
(5 minutes)

6. **Create Anticipation:**

NEXT WEEK
(5 minutes)

7. **Prayer:**

PRAYER
(10 minutes)

PLANNING PAGES FOR UNIT THREE

BEFORE THE SESSION

1. Complete all five days of the unit during your daily quiet times.

2. Pray, asking the Spirit's guidance for the session. Be right with God, confessing any known sin, so you may be a pure vessel for Him to use, excited to share truth. Pray for each group member.

3. Study each section with the magnifying glass icon. Identify from this section a few points for group discussion.

4. Prepare specifics for leading the session by filling in the "During the Session" page for the unit at right. Adapt the suggested segments to your group's needs.

5. Attend to any logistical issues, such as arranging the meeting place, posting signs, planning for refreshments, contacting group members, or gathering needed materials.

6. Make your own checklist:

During the Session

(Refer to page 147 for suggestions for using this page)

1. Welcome/Prayer:

   Prayer Requests:

WELCOME
AND PRAYER
(10 minutes)

2. Questions/Insights from Testimonies:

TESTIMONIES
(5 minutes)

3. Major Truths of Study:

TRUTHS
(10 minutes)

4. Discussion Questions Drawn from Study:

QUESTIONS
(15 minutes)

5. Summary/Challenge:

SUMMARY &
CHALLENGE
(5 minutes)

6. Create Anticipation:

NEXT WEEK
(5 minutes)

7. Prayer:

PRAYER
(10 minutes)

PLANNING PAGES FOR UNIT FOUR

BEFORE THE SESSION

1. Complete all five days of the unit during your daily quiet times.

2. Pray, asking the Spirit's guidance for the session. Be right with God, confessing any known sin, so you may be a pure vessel for Him to use, excited to share truth. Pray for each group member.

3. Study each section with the magnifying glass icon. Identify from this section a few points for group discussion.

4. Prepare specifics for leading the session by filling in the "During the Session" page for the unit at right. Adapt the suggested segments to your group's needs.

5. Attend to any logistical issues, such as arranging the meeting place, posting signs, planning for refreshments, contacting group members, or gathering needed materials.

6. Make your own checklist:

During the Session

(Refer to page 147 for suggestions for using this page)

1. Welcome/Prayer:

    Prayer Requests:

WELCOME
AND PRAYER
(10 minutes)

2. Questions/Insights from Testimonies:

TESTIMONIES
(5 minutes)

3. Major Truths of Study:

TRUTHS
(10 minutes)

4. Discussion Questions Drawn from Study:

QUESTIONS
(15 minutes)

5. Summary/Challenge:

SUMMARY &
CHALLENGE
(5 minutes)

6. Create Anticipation:

NEXT WEEK
(5 minutes)

7. Prayer:

PRAYER
(10 minutes)

BEFORE THE SESSION

1. Complete all five days of the unit during your daily quiet times.

2. Pray, asking the Spirit's guidance for the session. Be right with God, confessing any known sin, so you may be a pure vessel for Him to use, excited to share truth. Pray for each group member.

3. Study each section with the magnifying glass icon. Identify from this section a few points for group discussion.

4. Prepare specifics for leading the session by filling in the "During the Session" page for the unit at right. Adapt the suggested segments to your group's needs.

5. Attend to any logistical issues, such as arranging the meeting place, posting signs, planning for refreshments, contacting group members, or gathering needed materials.

6. Make your own checklist:

DURING THE SESSION

(Refer to page 147 for suggestions for using this page)

1. Welcome/Prayer:

    Prayer Requests:

WELCOME
AND PRAYER
(10 minutes)

2. Questions/Insights from Testimonies:

TESTIMONIES
(5 minutes)

3. Major Truths of Study:

TRUTHS
(10 minutes)

4. Discussion Questions Drawn from Study:

QUESTIONS
(15 minutes)

5. Summary/Challenge:

SUMMARY &
CHALLENGE
(5 minutes)

6. Create Anticipation:

NEXT WEEK
(5 minutes)

7. Prayer:

PRAYER
(10 minutes)

PLANNING PAGES FOR UNIT SIX

BEFORE THE SESSION

1. Complete all five days of the unit during your daily quiet times.

2. Pray, asking the Spirit's guidance for the session. Be right with God, confessing any known sin, so you may be a pure vessel for Him to use, excited to share truth. Pray for each group member.

3. Study each section with the magnifying glass icon. Identify from this section a few points for group discussion.

4. Prepare specifics for leading the session by filling in the "During the Session" page for the unit at right. Adapt the suggested segments to your group's needs.

5. Attend to any logistical issues, such as arranging the meeting place, posting signs, planning for refreshments, contacting group members, or gathering needed materials.

6. Make your own checklist:

DURING THE SESSION

(Refer to page 147 for suggestions for using this page)

1. Welcome/Prayer:

    Prayer Requests:

WELCOME
AND PRAYER
(10 minutes)

2. Questions/Insights from Testimony (Unit 6 has one testimony. Use the extra time for the workbook's conclusion.)**:**

TESTIMONY
(5 minutes)

3. Major Truths of Study:

TRUTHS
(10 minutes)

4. Discussion Questions Drawn from Study:

QUESTIONS
(15 minutes)

5. Summary/Challenge:

SUMMARY &
CHALLENGE
(5 minutes)

6. Evaluate the experience:

EVALUATE
(5 minutes)

7. Prayer:

PRAYER
(10 minutes)

Blackaby TITLES

Experiencing God
revised paperback
0-8054-0197-0
$12.99
revised hardcover
0-8054-0196-2
$16.99
audio
0-8054-1150-X
$15.99

*Experiencing God
Day-by-Day Devotional*
0-8054-1776-1
$14.99

*Experiencing God
Day-by-Day Devotional
and Journal*
0-8054-6298-8
$19.99

Experiencing God Together
0-8054-2481-4
$19.99

*Reflections on the Seven
Realities of Experiencing God*
0-8054-3779-7
$12.99

*The Experience
Day-by-Day Devotional
and Journal*
0-8054-1846-6
$19.99

*On Mission
With God*
0-8054-2553-5
$19.99

The Man God Uses
0-8054-2145-9
$15.99

*The Man God Uses
Devotional Journal*
0-8054-3526-3
$14.99

The Ways of God
0-8054-2373-7
$17.99

Spiritual Leadership
0-8054-1845-8
$19.99

Fresh Encounter
0-8054-6368-2
$17.99

The Power of the Call
0-8054-6297-X
$19.99

COMING SOON!

FROM *Best-selling author Henry Blackaby*

Hearing God's Voice
0-8054-2493-8
$17.99

BROADMAN
& HOLMAN
PUBLISHERS